Down To Earth

To Crew and Colleagues
in British Airways

Down To Earth

*The Courageous story of the
British Airways Stewardess
who Built an Orphanage in
Bangladesh*

PAT KERR
with Susan Hill

EBURY PRESS
LONDON

First published 1992 by Ebury Press
an imprint of the Random Century Group
Random Century House
20 Vauxhall Bridge Road
London SW1V 2SA

Catalogue record for this book is available
from the British Library.

ISBN 0 09 175159 4

Designed by Oliver Hickey

Typeset in Palatino by
Hope Services (Abingdon) Ltd
Printed and bound in Great Britain by
Mackays of Chatham plc, Kent

Contents

FOREWORD BY LORD KING   vii

ACKNOWLEDGEMENTS   ix

PROLOGUE   xi

Introduction – *What Am I Doing Here?*   1

1   Taking Wing   2

2   Indira Road   10

3   Descent to Dhaka   18

4   Families For Children   27

5   Raising The Roof   33

6   Building Work   43

7   A Visit to The President's Wife   50

8   The Move to Sreepur   55

9   Claire and Mark   64

10 Teething Troubles   70

11 A Life in A Day   77

12 Time Out   87

13	The Cost of Living	93
14	High Days	101
15	Shohel	105
16	The Real Rewards	110
17	The Fame Game	116
18	Monika	124
19	The Riot	131
20	Rina and Shopna	135
21	The Cyclone	139
22	What Next?	147
	Index	177

Foreword

LORD KING OF WARTNABY
CHAIRMAN
BRITISH AIRWAYS PLC

This book is a story of human suffering and human achievement. It is also the personal narrative of a wonderful young woman who wandered – almost by chance – into a situation of desperate social deprivation and did something about it.

Bangladesh is one of the poorest countries in the world. Over-populated and under-fed, millions of its citizens struggle to survive in conditions which would shock a modern-day Charles Dickens. In this mass of under-privileged and hungry people, the least favoured, most needy, of all are the children.

In 1981 Pat Kerr, a British Airways stewardess, began to work as a part-time volunteer at an overcrowded city-centre orphanage in down-town Dhaka. Other colleagues followed her example. The company was pleased to give support to their efforts. The story of their work was spread by a sympathetic media to readers and viewers all over the United Kingdom.

In 1989 the President of Bangladesh opened a splendid new children's village outside the village of Sreepur. The construction and equipment of the children's village had been financed almost entirely by voluntary contributions from people and companies anxious to support the work of Pat and her friends.

We live in an age when people talk a great deal

about caring but do not seem to do very much. The title of this book is very carefully chosen. Pat is at pains to stress that she is no Mother Teresa. She does not come from a religious background. When she joined British Airways she was motivated by 'the old hippy longing for the trail'. She loves her friends and values her social life. At times she has resented the claims on her of 600 children when she might have been caring for those of her own. Repeatedly Pat insists that she is no saint. That may be so. But in a wretched and disorganized world she has been involved in an heroic and inspired enterprise which, however human and imperfect, has been undeniably good. If that is not saintly it is close enough for me.

Acknowledgements

*I would like to thank the following people
who made it all possible.*

Gerry Devereux, Trish Silvester, Lord King of Wartnaby, Maura McDonagh, Airdrie Terenghi, George Bell, Rob Jenkinson, Andrea Bennett, Debby Vine, Inner Wheel Clubs, Round Tables, Rotary Clubs, British Press, 'The Visit Team' and the camera men and engineers that worked with them, Ron Scobling, Howard Phelps, Ted Gosling, Dr Frank Preston, Tony Galbraith, Bob Hammond, Gordon Bowden, Friends of Bangladesh, Bangladesh Women's Association, Tony Hickson, Sir Frank Kennedy, Dr Georgiades, Andy Muat, Peter Ryan, Bob Dunbar, Ron Selby, Rosie Walters, Bob Clarke, Alan McGill, Bob McLeod, Aruna Bhatia, Belinda Fraser, Michael Bell, Andy Dill, Tommy Miah, Camilla Alphonso, John Cater, Colin Varndell, Eileen Meadows, Janet Cassidy, George Peel, Jane Johnson, Louise Bell, Sue Tunnicliffe, Liz Ringwald, Ted Smart, Jim Berwick, Dr Mohtihar, Branwen Edwards, Christine Quick, Adrian Meredith, Ernie Reardon, Gwilym Rees Jones, Judith Phillips, Paul Murray, Rakesh Kochar, John Ackland, Mike Clough, Brigitte Krafczyk-Myers, Tony Howard Harrison, Peta Linlithgow, Beverly Swift, Malcolm Walker, Maureen King, Marz Lakdawalla, Dr MA Fazal, Alan Rowlands, Pauline Stamford, Rene Benson, Ranjit Bhumura, Olwen Haslam, Stan Havill, Shin Shinmar, Tim Woods, Trish Mckee, Charlie Sneddon, Ursula Murray, Zaf Khan, Jackie Harris, Mervyn Edwards, Gay Parson, Rashna Masters, Pat Dreusicke, Liz Glibbery, Sheila Mitchell, Maureen Fox, The Effingham Fund Raising Committee, Valerie Searle, Sheena Packham, Susan Godwin, Adrian Merrett, Lesley Robinson, Andrea Wright, Mishi Bellamy, Muhru Dimshaw.

On the building team

Godfrey Crook, Kamal Islam, Peter Wells, Trevor Williams, Martin Hurley, Dicken Adams, John Lowry, Peter Wilkes, David Tidnam, Ronald Taylor, William Foyle, Christopher Cooper-King, Shafiqul Islam, S. Chowdrey, Azmat Ulla, NC Das

BA Managers in Bangladesh

Ian Reid, Roy Barnes, John and Di Emery, Mike and Dawn Osborn

High Commissioners

Sir Terrence and Lady Streeton, HE Mr C. Imray and Mrs S. Imray.

In Bangladesh

British Women's Association, United Nations Women's Association, United Kingdom Association of Bangladesh and all the expatriate groups and individuals who have helped us so much.

Mr Wajid Ali Khan Panni, Mr Farook Ahmed, Mr Azizur Rahman, Suzette Haque, Mr Mustapha Jabbar, Mr Rofique, Chris Price, Brother Donald Becker, Father George Pope, Terres Des Hommes, Ubinig, Proshika, Mennonite Central Committee, Gonoshassthaya Kendra, Concern, Save the Children, Oxfam, ODA, VSD, CIDA.

For the book

Susan Hill, Rowena Webb, Lucinda Culpin, Trish Silvester, Liz Glibbery, Audrey O'Neill, Patrick McCreeth, and Brenda Glover.

For tolerating me

My parents, brother and sister – Wing Commander and Mrs HR Kerr, Iain Kerr and Vivienne Rogan.

Many thanks to everybody else who helped. The names above are those I gathered together during the final stages of preparing the book. They are in no particular order and I deeply apologise to all those wonderful people I have unintentionally left out.

Prologue

There were a number of reasons for writing this book, the obvious and most important one being to interest people in the children and the charity. It has also been an opportunity for me to give a personal view of many wonderful as well as sad experiences in a culture very different from my own. The development environment is, rightly, dominated by people with appropriate academic backgrounds and it is only fair to say that any opinions given are purely personal and not based on statistics or formal research. This is very much a subjective recounting of a series of events that led me and about eight hundred other people to live in a 'Children's Village' in rural Bangladesh.

I have found it challenging to write. This stems partially from the fact that the qualities and skills that make me any good at running a project in Bangladesh make me very bad at describing it. To cope from day to day I have learnt to minimise any drama, reduce all situations to the fundamentals of 'what can be done'. To adequately describe things here so they can be understood in the comparative comfort in which it will mostly be read, I have found very difficult. Dealing with situations is a sort of refuge from thinking about an often overwhelming reality, remembering incidents and writing about them is not.

Being involved in a project that has totally dominated my life for over ten years has been a great privilege. Almost everybody is happier when engaged in an undertaking they see as greater than themselves, whether it's building up a business, bringing up a family or working for a charity. This probably applies even more to those of us who have no religious beliefs. The frequently announced problems of the rich and famous show that those two things alone are not enough to bring contentment. Whilst I would not advocate people rushing off to engage themselves in dramatic projects I hope that this book shows the personal benefits that this involvement has brought me.

I hope you will enjoy reading about what happened. I hope you will feel like helping the children in it but more than anything else I hope that a few people will read the story and realise that in their own way they can make a difference. Having been happily and consistently average throughout school and adult life I saw an opportunity and decided to get out there and do something. We're all involved with each other and with our increasingly fragile environment and we haven't time to wait for saints or politicians to sort the world out for us.

'Nobody made a greater mistake than he who did nothing because he could only do a little.'

EDMUND BURKE

Introduction
What Am I Doing Here?

Walking in mud, slimy and high above my knees. When my toes felt something solid that my feet could rest on for a second I was both relieved and horrified. For all I knew, I could have been balancing on a corpse. It was better not to think too much and to wade on towards the boat. We were on a flooded mudflat, just after the cyclone of April 1991, and I'd seen the photographs of the hundreds of bodies washed up on this coast.

No one quite knows the exact population of Bangladesh – partly because the registration of births is a little casual – but it is somewhere between 120 million and 150 million. The habitable landmass is roughly the size of Wales. This poor, new, under-funded and misunderstood nation was simply experiencing the latest tragedy in a recent history of flood, famine, war, pestilence and indifference, and there wasn't even a way to afford simple human dignity to those who survived. It wasn't up to me, or the team of which I was part, to ponder these horrors as we tried to reach an area of damp – not dry – land where people might want our basic first-aid skills, supplies and advice.

Most experts believe that at least 150,000 people died in the spring cyclone of 1991.

Entire villages and communities had been obliterated, fragile mud-constructed houses were blown apart,

1

crop fields were flooded and basic services like village telephones, electricity links and decent drinking water had gone. Drugs were needed to cope with the sort of infections that set in so fast in conditions like this, and aid agencies all over the world were rushing relief into the area.

So what was I doing here wading in mud?

1

Taking Wing

Because I'm working with children in Bangladesh I've been called a saint, an angel and another Mother Teresa more times than I can count, and I hate it. I started helping in Bangladesh for selfish reasons: I was doing it for me – I wasn't driven by altruism or conscience beyond any normal human compassion. Anyway, I meet a lot of incredible people who do much more than I'd ever think of.

The best example is a British woman called Valerie Taylor, who has lived in Bangladesh for some twenty-two years. Valerie, a physiotherapist, runs a project for the disabled in Savar, which is on the other side of Dhaka. Over the last thirteen years the Centre for the Rehabilitation of the Paralysed has cared for over a thousand people from all over Bangladesh. They have been given shelter, treatment and rehabilitation and have been taught skills which enable them to earn their own living. Dressmakers, civil servants, an MP and shoe cleaners are among people whose childhood spinal injuries consigned them to the scrap heap of life before they were rescued at the hands of Valerie's centre. She has adopted two lovely little girls who suffer from cerebral palsy and has selflessly and quietly worked to help disabled people in Bangladesh to achieve their highest possible potential.

Compared with Valerie, I have a pretty easy time. She is always struggling to fund her wonderful work, whereas, although we too have problems, we have benefited from a great deal of publicity. I love my job at Sreepur but I don't want to do it for ever, any more than I wanted to fly for British Airways for ever. I loved that job, too, but when I went to Bangladesh I felt it was time for a change.

Even when I was a child, change – of scene, at any rate – was a constant part of my life. My father Harry, who is now in his seventies, retired early from the RAF as a wing commander. We went to live in my mother's village of Lostwithiel in Cornwall, where he took over a long-established family grocery business and we moved into my grandparents' large house on a hill. Until then the three of us children – me, my sister Vivienne and brother Iain – had moved around a lot, as service families do, and had been to school all over the world. Before moving to Cornwall in the sixties we'd been in California for three years, and before that in Ireland.

I liked travelling but was happy to be in Lostwithiel in that lovely shambling house with my grandparents around. I went to a local grammar school, while Vivienne, and later Iain, went to boarding schools. My mother Rosemary had grown up in the village and still seemed to know everyone. She was soon involved in various community activities, including the running of the tiny branch library, but although both my parents are kind and caring people no religious or moral pressure was ever put upon any of us. Vivienne became a nurse and Iain works for an American green organization concerned with whale preservation. And me?

Well, it's all pretty unremarkable. I left grammar school after a year in the sixth form to begin a three-year course in Exeter, training as an occupational therapist. After Lostwithiel, which is a charming place but deathly quiet for teenagers, Exeter seemed like the height of sophisticated bohemia. My college was an old-fashioned exception. Even then, in the late sixties, the girls had to address each other as Miss This or Miss That even if they were sharing a room, and we were fined if there was a ladder in our stockings. It really was stiflingly formal. I was the students' social secretary and had to get permission for late-night passes for dances. In fact, involvement in a minor rebellion over accommodation almost got me expelled!

The course was well devised, though. We were made to try and get some experience of many different types of jobs and lifestyles and some understanding of various handicaps and disabilities. For instance, we had to cook a meal from a wheelchair, spend a day with our dominant arm in a sling – that sort of thing. After I qualified I wanted to work with drug-dependent people. An idealistic desire to learn about their problems at grass-roots level made me take a job as a house mother in a community for registered addicts in Hackney, east London. I left after six weeks when I was attacked by someone and ended up in hospital with concussion. I figured I'd learned enough from that side.

I then got a job as an occupational therapist in a rehabilitation unit attached to the Royal Maudsley Hospital in south London. Once my plan to have a wholesome little picnic degenerated into a field search for magic mushrooms. Later I transferred to a general psychiatric unit, but didn't find it very challenging, and so I started looking around for something else.

I applied to do VSO (Voluntary Service Overseas) but was turned down. Looking back, I'm pleased. At twenty-two I was too immature and idealistic to have been particularly useful. So there was a passage of time in London when I wafted around in my cheesecloth blouses and long skirts, carrying, for a while, a little brass bowl instead of a handbag. I worked for some friends who restored harpsichords in Marylebone, and had occasional jobs as a waitress and a shop assistant.

From this unlikely situation I applied to BOAC, as

it was then. The idea of being a stewardess seemed to embrace both the old hippy longing for the trail and my more conventional wish to travel again. It seemed a good way to see the world for free. Before British Airways came into being there were two national airlines – BEA for European flights and BOAC for long hauls. I applied to BOAC, as I wanted to travel to as many exotic places as I could.

My family were fondly dismissive. Me? For a start I was famously clumsy, and wasn't my long-haired, ethnic, flower-child look somewhat at variance with the coolly groomed, neatly suited air stewardess image? I was granted an interview, however (of course, they'd never seen me in my hippy splendour), and my mother came to London to give me practical and moral support. We went to Barker's in Kensington – next door to what became the big Biba, where I later had another short-lived part-time job in the children's department – and bought a neat little suit. It was a black and white tweed job with a leather trim. I wish I'd kept it. Later, working at Biba and having, to everyone's astonishment, been accepted by BOAC, I learned that quite a few of those sultry, poised Biba girls had also applied. This made me all the more astonished that I'd been offered a chance. My family's amazement was the most fun of all.

Halfway through the terrifying interview I was sure that all was lost, and I stopped worrying too much. So many people had told me I wouldn't get in, I wasn't that optimistic anyway. Finally, relieved that my ordeal was over, I shook the hand of the woman who had interviewed me, thanked her and said how much I had enjoyed our conversation. In retrospect I'm sure that was why they offered me a place – I had finally redeemed myself by a little display of spontaneous manners and an ability to address her as a person. I think they were looking for people who, during a long and fractious flight, could show concern and interest in other people.

The training, six weeks of it, was at Heathrow. At the time I was living with my sister Vivienne, in Hammersmith, and our flat-mates were typically rampageous medical students. We had a lot of fun; once one of them dared me to put an advertisement in the lonely hearts column of the then new London magazine, *Time Out*. 'Stewardess wants to meet interesting people. . . '. I got over six hundred replies, some fascinating, some weird and some sad. It did strike me, though, that the word 'stewardess' may be as potent as 'voluptuous' or 'adventurous' if you're thinking of composing a small ad. I now often quite resent my new image as a do-gooder – it's led to a real deterioration in my social life!

I felt I was making a total mess of my training. Everyone else seemed so much more self-possessed than me, and I found everything a terrible strain – from the Elizabeth Arden beauty lessons to deportment classes with a book on my head. I was used to a much more relaxed appearance than the little bandbox mini-suits and forage caps, the groomed hair and all the niceties of hostessing. I learned afterwards, and with no surprise, that my early assessments had been pretty bad.

When I finally started to fly I had trouble with small talk and unfamiliar currencies in equal measure. I didn't feel I was performing my principal duty – that of placing passengers at their ease – terribly well. In fact I muddled through it all in misery, and often thought of packing it up. I was OK about being welcoming and hospitable and had stopped worrying too much about spilling coffee or drinks, but for the first few months I was uncomfortable and wretched and only hung in because I still loved the idea of travel and wanted to see as many places as possible. It was quite a long time before I was able to overcome my feelings of shyness and inadequacy and feel comfortable with fellow crew members on stopovers. It seems crazy now when I remember how nervous I was, but even today public engagements and the things I have to do to get publicity for the charity still terrify me. Still, I've come a long way from being too nervous to pick up the phone and speak to the stewardess in the next room to see if she felt like a coffee.

Eventually I loosened up, and then I started to enjoy the extroverted, sometimes crazy, times with crews. When I look at my photo albums now I see endless groups of flight crews, some at touristy places but lots in restaurants and bars all round the world. Tables are scattered with the cheerful debris of some exotic meal or other, bottles, overflowing ashtrays. . . . In that curious red-eye flash photographic look we all seem to be happy aliens – which, I suppose, we were in a way. There was always a fantastic little place – and word was passed from crew to crew – where you could party as late and as long as you wanted to. Sometimes I barely recognize myself in the pictures. Hair a different length or style, some deeply unsuitable blouse, arms round this crew member or that. By the late seventies you could certainly say that I'd got into the swing of things, and was enjoying both my work on the aircraft and the sociability that every flight crew enjoys during the weeks they are together.

It's a very curious existence. Flight crews work intensively during the journey, but might then have long periods waiting in a hotel before going back on duty. Strong camaraderie can be forged during a long-haul flight, particularly if it has been in any way a tricky one, so relaxing with colleagues is both natural and necessary. If the flight was to Sydney, say, you'd have a day in the Middle East and then a day or two in Singapore to rest before going on to Australia, where you'd be off duty for another day or so. You might fly back via Delhi and Hong Kong or other pleasant stopovers before you reached London. That particular nucleus of staff might never work together again, but we would learn to enjoy each other's company very much for those two or three weeks that we were working together. Unless you had relatives anywhere, it was pretty much inevitable that your free time would be spent with your colleagues.

It was charmed in its way. I knew it then, and I think fondly of it now. All that duty-free, irresponsible fun. We all worked very hard for short, intense periods whilst we were flying, and then enjoyed equally serious relaxation. Often we'd want to see 'sights' and get some sense of the country we were staying in, and a group of us would hire a car for the day and just enjoy being tourists.

Around this time I wanted to get a base in London. I'd lived with friends near Baker Street, with Vivienne in Hammersmith, with a boyfriend in Woking – and now I needed a bolt-hole of my own. I'd bought a place in Woking, but for various reasons I wanted out. After staying with a dear friend, Adrian, in Chiswick for a while I realized that this was the area I'd like to live in. I found a derelict ground-floor flat just over the road from Gunnersbury Station. It had a tiny garden – very important to me – and this mitigated against its horrific internal disorder. For some while I lived in one room, eating pizza and pitta bread, drinking red wine and surrounded by chaos. I don't know what it says about me that the first step towards home improvement was the purchase of a dishwasher. Gradually I have come to regard it as a real home – somewhere that I can collapse into whenever I'm back in England.

It's very handy for the airport. I have a sunny living room, two good-sized bedrooms, the usual facilities and a little patch of grass outside. The street is quiet, leafy and lined with comfortably bulky Edwardian terraced houses. It doesn't take much to understand why this place is so important to me. It is peaceful, with modest, civilized comforts that don't yet exist in Bangladesh. And it reminds me, if I should ever need such reminders, that my plain little room in Sreepur does not represent and sum up the whole of my life.

I hope it will now be clear that I don't fit any saintly role more usually given to people in my line of work. I've grabbed opportunities, experimented with different kinds of lifestyles, relationships, politics and ideas. Flying was great, and I enjoyed it for as long as I could. The fact that I came to feel such admiration and affection for so many of my colleagues was not something that I anticipated. However, in fairness to that naive flower-child, I see now that something of her philosophy lingered throughout all the roaring times in night clubs and restaurants. I was always struck by great temples and majestic landscapes as well as by the newest hot-spot. It was never a chore or a bore for me to listen to other people's points of view or explanations. I always wanted to know more about the country whose guest I was. Perhaps I always had a wish to be part of different places and perhaps to help in some way. It's hard now to be sure about seeds that might have been sown long ago. . . .

Although the lifestyle is very different, I have no problem in relating what I do now to what I did then. It is simply a turn of events. It never was, and isn't now, a matter of giving up a frivolous life to do good, but certainly a little of that old hippy 'one world' idealism got packed up in a suitcase along with my smart uniform. That got combined with an urgent personal desire to make the most of the life I have and a hope that I might leave behind some positive feelings. There was also, of course, the brilliant example set by my parents – a kind of do-as-you-would-be-done-by automatic graceful kindness.

2

Indira Road

I've never really understood what the difference is between fate and destiny. People often speak of them as if they were different and opposing forces, the one self-ordained and the other self-determined. I find it easier to grasp the notions embodied in the old maxim that luck is where opportunity meets preparation. Whatever, I certainly do believe that momentous turns in our lives can be made through events that may seem trivial at the time, and only in retrospect is the significance sometimes revealed.

There's a bus queue theory. You've been waiting for a number 19 for nearly half an hour now and you're late for a meeting. Do you refuse to cut your losses, throw more good time after bad and pray that the number 19 will wheel round the corner before you've counted ten red hatchbacks? Or do you think: Hell, I'll walk? And if you walk, might you run into an old friend who will then introduce you to someone who will change your life? Might you step into a shop and buy a paper that has the job of your dreams advertised in its back pages? Equally, you might just slip and break your ankle.

I believe that some of our crassest decisions can shape our lives; you could meet that friend, pick up that paper and even slip on the bus. This is a dilemma that I have yet to resolve – but I'll be a happy woman when I can. In the meantime I remember what someone said to me hundreds of years ago: in life one will always collect a few regrets, and it is better to regret the things you did rather than the things you didn't do. For me, this is an essential ethos.

One morning I woke up in a hotel in Dhaka to find some grand schemes and a hangover having a boxing match in my head. The night before, bewailing the fact that it was the middle of the monsoon season and that trips and expeditions were out of the question, the crew I was with had cursed their luck about being assigned this flight. In the early eighties, BA flew regularly to Dhaka. It was part of a longish tour that stopped over in some exotic Far Eastern places. The Dhaka stopover was not regarded as the high point of the tour, even though we stayed, as ever, in a lovely hotel with a pool, good restaurants and all the usual comforts.

We moaned cheerfully for about half an hour, had another beer and adjusted the air conditioning. Then one crew member – known for his outrageous sense of humour – became uncharacteristically serious. What on earth, he said, gave us the right to complain? We were cool, dry, well fed and well cared for. People on the road from the airport who had happily waved to our bus on its way to the hotel would go home to shacks at best, where the wet and the dirt and the overcrowding and the squalor would be impossible for any of us to endure for a single night, let alone every single night. So what did it matter if we couldn't go shopping in the morning?

The room became silent, and at last someone said that on their last trip to Bombay they had visited one of Mother Teresa's homes. We started talking about practical things that we might do – bringing in clothes and medicines, and helping in some way during stopovers. Other BA staff had spent time working on projects in

Egypt and Sri Lanka. There wasn't any reason why we couldn't try and do a bit here.

When I was training as a therapist I had been warned that I should control my 'enthusiasms'. It wasn't that I was being deterred from real, valuable work, but that I was too much of an idealist and shouldn't get carried away. Of course I was infuriated by these admonitions and self-righteous enough to resent anyone telling me how to manage my ideals. But in the early eighties I understood that ideals and enthusiasms are no good without commitment and action. Now I started to feel an 'enthusiasm' coming on, and dominated the conversation for the rest of the evening. I grabbed some hotel stationery and started to make some lists – always a good start – of what we could do and how we could begin.

Firstly we needed to contact a place that could use our help, where they spoke English and where people like us who could only flash in and out of the country every so often could be genuinely useful. I planned to call the British Airways office in Dhaka in the morning and seek advice. One of the other girls, Evelyn, said she'd speak to a friend of hers at the Canadian High Commission. The talk went on and eventually all of us, sleepy, slightly drunk on beer and fired by idealism, drifted off to our rooms.

I couldn't sleep, and continued drafting notes until three in the morning. I felt gripped by the possibilities; I enjoyed offering blankets and hot drinks to elderly passengers who couldn't sleep on long-haul flights, but I wanted to do a bit more.

I was painfully reminded of a charged moment in a recent relationship. A former boyfriend had mentioned a pile-up on the motorway in which six people had just died. My response was that this must be the explanation why I'd been about an hour late for our date – I'd been stuck in traffic and fuming. With cold accuracy he had informed me that it was pretty dreadful if I could only see this ghastly tragedy in terms of one corpse for each ten minutes that I had been so tiresomely delayed. It was hurtful, but shaming and true. Last night's conversation had been along very similar lines, and I was determined that we, or at least I, should do something practical after that late-night discussion and not consign it to the dustbin of a hundred other earnest and idealistic supper ramblings.

Eventually I slept. I've always had trouble with time zones – bad news for an airline stewardess – and it wasn't until noon the next day that I woke up. Stumbling towards the shower, I saw that a couple of notes had been pushed under my door. Evelyn had already contacted her friend at the High Commission and a meeting had been set up for one o'clock. He was going to show us a small project and discuss things. What a mouth I must have seemed, I thought, as I showered, clambered into some clothes, rang BA, abandoned any thoughts of breakfast or lunch, grabbed last night's notes, rushed to the lift and met the others in the lobby. I tolerated the inevitable teasing and banter. Anyway, that's how it all started.

Next day, the three of us careered through the streets in our rickshaw, having negotiated the fare beforehand, as you must. We were on our way to Indira Road, to the headquarters of Families For Children. I remember the heavy presence of rain in the air, the colours and the noise as we tacked from street to street. It wasn't my first trip through the streets of Dhaka, but this time I was acutely aware of the poverty in the streets, the social conditions that generate the disease and squalor that people here have to endure so passively. Even so, I was overwhelmed as never before by the gaiety and energy of the city. It's like a fairground, with the same cheerful sense of impermanence and the same brash, brassy front. People talk about the street life in cities like New York, but the busy clamour of downtown Dhaka at lunchtime is hard to beat.

Today we only dodge buses. Later I frequently

travelled on them. In this part of the world it's the most common form of transport. Timetables and schedules are chaotic, but sooner or later one of them will show up. The buses are beat-up old coaches and Britain's five-standing-only rule certainly doesn't apply. A coach built for thirty passengers will usually carry sixty or more with many of them clinging to the roof, and the running boards, and seemingly tipping out of the windows. Ancient as they are, the clapped-out old warhorses cover the dusty, often rutted miles at a terrifying lick. There is, nevertheless, a curious formal observance of bus stops, so much so that there is invariably a little cluster of shabby shops near the spot where the bus is known to pause.

A bus ride is a pretty uncomfortable experience for a woman on her own, especially a foreigner. Within that crush a certain amount of pressing and heaving is inevitable. There's a special area at the front for women, but it still provides a sort of open season for fumblings and pinching as the men get on and off.

An alternative is something called a baby taxi. They are little three-wheeled mini-moke affairs decorated as brightly as totem poles, and they buzz you through the city for pennies. More common still are the bicycle rickshaws such as we were in on this particular day – also gaudily painted and operated by men apparently so frail that they don't look able to lift a brick, let alone pull along some of the loads they do. I gather the life expectancy of the rickshaw drivers is pretty low, and when I watch them at work I'm not surprised. Hauling along the 'cab' with one slightish passenger like me is one thing but often – again, as on this day – there are as many as five adults crammed into the back. Sometimes the cab is detached and a kind of cart is fixed to the back instead so that they can undertake more 'industrial' work. For all I know they could be pulling sacks of feathers, but I think it more likely that they are heaving great loads of grain or building materials. Anyone who in the past ever felt sorry

15

for an English dray horse and wondered how they coped with their burdens would be astonished and appalled to see the loads tugged by the bicycle rickshaw drivers of Dhaka.

The road we were taking to the FFC was bumpy, and the seat uncomfortable. Horns blared, people ran across the road and it was as dizzying as a fairground ride. We stopped at some lights. This isn't at all common in Dhaka, where drivers tend to sail gaily through and hope for the best. But a policeman had flagged us down this time, so the driver had to pause. A woman who looked about forty but was probably only in her twenties approached the rickshaw, holding up her baby. She smiled and asked for baksheesh. I fumbled in my bag for change, but by then the lights were changing. I could only smile and pat the baby's head before we raced off. The mother smiled and the baby gurgled. This is so typical of Bangladesh: some people do beg, but they beg in an inoffensive, unthreatening way. They still smile even if you can't find the money. Their patience and calm are heartbreaking.

The FFC headquarters was in a narrow road near the Parliament buildings – but don't be misled by this. In Dhaka a palatial house often abuts a tin shed or a sweatshop. The rickshaw driver negotiated the gates with difficulty and much shouting at other drivers in the lane. The building was Victorian, and damp had caused moss to flourish on the outer walls. The small courtyard was overgrown with lush plants, and the overall effect was somehow dignified and pleasing. It had just started to rain heavily, so we paid the driver and rushed inside. The bill for the ride, for all three of us, was less than I would have paid for a coffee in the hotel.

Indoors there was an air of calm and competence. Two women were dealing with paperwork on large refectory-type tables and we were surrounded by the unmistakable detritus of babies. Steaming nappies, toys and clothes: not mess, but certainly that distinct baby smell. We were introduced to two Canadians, Betty Steinkraus and Sherrell Judish. They were running the place, and thought now would be a good time for us to have a look round as most of the 150 babies were sleeping.

As we did so, Betty told us something about the origins of Families For Children. It had been founded as a charity during the Vietnam War by two women who went out to adopt babies for themselves and ended up arranging adoptions for many others. They opened a refuge for children who did not find suitable adoptee parents. Sandra Simpson, Sherrell's sister, was one of the founders and is now president of the charity, running it from her home in Toronto.

FFC has no religious or political ties. It is a very small charity depending on the goodwill of people in Canada, the United States and Europe, particularly Britain and the Scandinavian countries. Funds tend to be raised privately.

As we walked round the place I was struck by the sight of all the tiny wooden cots. Some clearly disabled children were not sleeping but being watched by one or other of the ayahs – some of the mothers who stayed to help. The babies were minute, with oddly angled limbs and distended abdomens. I saw later that the care the very little ones received at Indira Road added weight and a gloss of health which helps protect them against future illnesses.

Then, to my alarm, a woman thrust a minute baby into my arms. I'd never, ever been too good with babies and this one was hardly the bouncing, cuddly, gurgling type, eager to be petted and squeezed. Her eyes were bleary and unfocussed, her skin wrinkled and old. I hugged her hesitantly, scared that I would hurt her, but she seemed too weak to react in any way. I felt very awkward. A different baby was thrust into my arms and the ayah seemed to be saying, 'Try again. Don't worry.

They're tough.' She took both back, rocked them expertly in her arms and chanted their names. I felt completely useless.

When we went downstairs the toddlers were waking up from their nap and made us welcome by totally engulfing us. The squealing, joyful, trusting affection offered by these children to complete strangers is terribly affecting and moving. They called all of us 'Mummy', plied us with questions in Bengali and sang little fragments of English nursery rhymes.

There's a danger that I'm making the place seem like some perfect haven of rest, peace and safety. In some ways it was (especially if you'd been living lately in a few plastic sheets and corrugated iron panels slung together by the side of a fetid river). But, just like any old period house, it was certainly in need of care and attention. The baby smell was one thing – the stench of damp and mould was another. Plaster was crumbling from the walls and a pervading odour of disinfectant, with a slight overlay of sick and pee, hung in the airless rooms.

Next we were briefly shown where the older children lived. Boys and girls had separate quarters. Some of the girls came up and were touchingly thrilled that their home was being visited. I noticed how beautiful they were and how fascinated they were with our watches, jewellery and clothes. Some of the girls were endearingly forward, informing me that I should do something about growing the fringe out of my shoulder-length, fairish hair. I thought it was extraordinary, considering the circumstances in which they had grown up, that these girls should be so cheerful and self-confident.

We went on to the school, a one-storey building which doubled as accommodation for the boys. It had a leaking corrugated iron roof and the lashing rain made the place thunderously noisy. How could anyone learn there, let alone sleep there? But Betty told me that by local standards everything was pretty good. The din was appalling, but the children had been used to much worse. It was almost dry. There were books, and plenty of paper to write or draw on. I had a lot of adjusting to do.

English was being taught as a second language, and although the schoolroom looked nothing like an English classroom, I could see that study was being taken seriously and that much was being achieved there. Some of the older boys grinned and spoke to me in fragmented English.

The tour was as good as over. We had tea in the dining room and were served with delicious cinnamon bread by Benjamin who, some years later, became the cook for the staff block at Sreepur. I was speechless, simultaneously impressed by what Betty and Sherrell were doing and appalled at the odds that they were working against. We discussed what BA crews might contribute to the project and agreed that we could easily bring over nappy-rash cream and ointments for scabies and lice. I nodded and agreed with all this, but was already wondering if I could do something more. They were saying that even people visiting to play with the babies would make things easier for the staff. . . .

However, for the time being we simply agreed to let it be known amongst British Airways staff that the FFC home existed, that it would welcome visitors, and that it would be thrilled to receive nappies and practical supplies. I said I'd write a piece about it for the staff magazine.

Then it was time to leave. In a moment of sublime irony we were collected in a limousine organized by the Canadian High Commission and a group of children gathered to see us off.

I thought the place was wonderful, and was already wondering how I could fix my schedules so that I could be in Dhaka as often as possible. I didn't then have the remotest intention of tipping my life into a completely new one. I had no idea that my attachment would grow or that I would become so deeply committed. I just thought that this would be a great place for us to do our bit and that it could be good for us and good for them.

'Come back. Come back. . . .' the children squealed as we left the alley.

3

Descent to Dhaka

The fact that even as a child I felt I had to make the most of every opportunity that was offered must say a lot about my parents, Harry and Rosemary. I don't remember much in the way of strict indoctrinations but I think they must have made it clear to us children that we were lucky to spend parts of our lives in somewhere as different and glamorous as California.

I can remember behaving really badly twice. When I was six or seven I cheated in a maths test at a very strict Irish school, and the person I copied from was punished. I feel guilty and horrible about that even now, but remember being too terrified of the teacher to own up. Another time my mother wouldn't give me any money so I pinched a ten-shilling note from her bag. I bought some chocolate or whatever I wanted and said that I had found the change on the beach in Scotland, where we lived at the time. Mother probably had a pretty sure idea of where I might have 'liberated' the ten-shilling note, so she marched me down to the police station and made me report the 'find' and hand in the change. I don't think I saw it again.

I am so lucky to have been brought up in an environment that didn't make me 'grow up' too quickly or even realize that the magic circle of my family could not protect me from the harsh realities of life. I had years of protected tranquillity, and only recently have I realized that the vast majority of children are born into situations where they have to struggle for survival as soon as they can think. My parents travelled and took us everywhere with them so we had security and new adventures at the same time. I was brought up to be honest and behave decently, and also not to let opportunities pass. I thought about this as I sat on a flight bound for Bangladesh – as a passenger for once, and not serving the supper.

Some old wish was about to be indulged without losing any of my securities at home. BA had given me unpaid leave of absence, so I knew that my job would be waiting for me when I wanted to return to flying. My boyfriend was not greatly impressed, but was tolerant. My parents were supportive. I was just off to have a break from myself and my old life. I had everything to come back to after indulging in a real adventure. In my own way I'd succeeded; most people, rightly, would call me unambitious, but I had tried to strike out. I was excited about actually going to live in an exotic and different country, even if only for a few months. Much as I had come to love flying I found the possibility of getting really entrenched in a strange culture, rather than literally skimming over its sunsets and landmarks, very appealing. Although I had flown there many times after the first visit to FFC, as a stewardess I seldom had time to look out of the windows and see Bangladesh as we touched down. Now I could.

You fly in from Bombay – it takes about three hours from there. The country is waterlogged and, depending on the season, is various shades of yellow or brown as you observe it from the sky. It seems flat, wet and featureless. Only when you touch land do you see the verdant woods and orchards, appreciate that those low-slung fishing boats are actually scudding along beautiful rivers and estuaries. From the air even the sea seems brown from the silt that the latest flood or monsoon has washed down the banks, taking a share of farming land with it.

By now, more than a year after my first visit, I'd been back and forth to Dhaka quite a lot. I'd carried heavy cases full of donated clothes and medicines. I'd heard about the wife and family of Benjamin, the cook. The children at FFC rushed up and called me 'Pat Mummy' instead of just 'Mummy'. I'd cuddled some little ones after scrapes and bruises, and broken up a few fights. I'd been drawn to the children and drawn into their way of life.

On the second visit, they'd been surprised to see me back, but after that demanded a return date before I was allowed to leave. Although still just a visitor, I felt part of the project. When I heard they needed volunteers for the winter of 1982, I didn't even have to think. I jumped at the chance – then went home to try and make it possible.

With the staunch support of Gerry Devereux, my manager at BA, I was ready to play a more serious part than that of the visiting godmother, someone who always arrived with bundles of goodies and left shortly afterwards with a wave and a promise. Gerry was marvellous. He thought it was a great thing for his crews to be involved with – and if the project obtained some favourable publicity, so much the better. Nine managers out of ten would have told me to get it all out of my system in my free time, and would have worried about how the larger commitment I wanted could have a detrimental effect on my function as a crew member. But Gerry immediately saw that, with careful thought and a constructive attitude, the crew, the airline and the children could benefit from this situation.

I was on my way towards a three-month stint as a volunteer. This time I would not be able to return to the hotel, after spending a few hours with the children, and relax in an immaculate bathroom afterwards. I wouldn't have the comforting knowledge that I could leave at a second's notice – and there was, for the time being, no money slipping into my bank account every month to pay for treats after a difficult day. I'd still have contact with BA crews when they visited the project, but I'd be living as well as working in the home in Dhaka.

Back home Peter, the man I lived with, had been unhappy about my decision. But we were very close, and he was a compassionate man who understood how important this was to me. He gave me a great deal of support, and we had planned and booked a splendid holiday to take together when my three months were up. I thought about him as the flight continued, hoping he'd like the surprise I'd left for him at the flat. It's always awful returning to an empty place if you're used to someone's presence, so on the day of my departure I'd gone out and bought an outrageous inflatable doll, blown her up and propped her against the pillows. I'd also found a first edition of one of his favourite books, by Kipling, and arranged this in her glossy plastic hands. I grinned as I thought of him walking into the room, and the likely expression on his face as he switched on the bedroom light and saw her.

The descent to Dhaka began. Rumour had it that I was doing this in some spirit of do-gooding and martyrdom: I'd become defensive about explaining that, far from it, I was doing it selfishly, for me. Although I did care, I was so fed up with this being seen as the only motive that whatever caring instincts I had were suppressed, and I constantly insisted that, whilst I liked working with the children well enough, the main point was to do something different, to experience another culture fully for a while.

However, there's no doubt that being cast, willy-nilly, as the all-purpose British Airways angel and tottering uneasily on that pedestal meant that my colleagues would be concerned and interested in the project. I was already looking forward to their visits. More and more crew members had started to call at the home, getting to know staff and children and bringing nappies, medicines and all sorts of other things which are hard to come by in Bangladesh. Some crew members didn't want to see the home, but brought supplies for it none the less. Thus a sort of benevolent relationship, almost possessiveness, had been forged. I was elated as we touched down. Participation, not mere observation, was what I had always wanted.

As a stewardess I had been spared the complexities of immigration at Dhaka. Crew members observe the formalities but they are brief. This time there was an interminable queue from a Tristar-load of passengers, and a baffled interchange with the customs people who were vaguely suspicious of my need for a case full of nappies. Four people or more tried to grab my luggage and harry me towards the taxi rank outside, but I was rescued by Mr J. K. Das, driver, handyman and general factotum who has worked for FFC for years. We headed off towards the doubty 1961 Vauxhall Victor where a group of squealing little girls, including my closest young friends, Rina and Shopna, formed a welcoming committee. All the girls fingered my hair as we drove jerkily through the city, giggling and crawling all over me. There was great excitement: 'Hello Pat Mummy', kisses and hugs. Exhausted after the flight, it was blissful to bask in this luxuriant charge of total acceptance and affection.

They chattered, their thin brown limbs in a tangle all around me, and I thought how different this unrestrained demonstrative informality was, from the stiffly controlled behaviour of most English children of similar ages. The fact that all this joy was coming from such socially bruised little ones made it all the more extraordinary. Such physical affection is common and natural and it's marvellous that they don't seem to have it stifled out of them. Perhaps in a poor society like this they really need that fearlessness and trust. Perhaps their ability to show, and receive, spontaneous fondness makes up a little for some of their deprivations. Their culture is much more family-orientated than that of the British. If you are fond of someone you call them 'aunt' or 'uncle' or 'mummy'. Being tactile comes naturally and physical affection is a wonderful luxury, freely indulged.

We arrived at the shadowy, overgrown courtyard of the house that was to become home to me. I was greeted by the girl I was to work with, Alison, and was immediately taken by her cheerful confidence. I'd been concerned earlier by what my fellow volunteers would be like and was relieved she seemed so nice. She didn't seem at all holy or prissy and – with a troop of girls following us – led me to the room we would be sharing. In retrospect I'm surprised I hadn't made enquiries about my accommodation, but maybe it was just as well I hadn't known. The room was barely big enough for two single beds; a wire stretched across one wall and strung with a few metal hangers, comprised the wardrobe. There were two small shelves between the ends of the beds and the wall.

Ever since I was eight years old I've had somewhere that was my private space, somewhere to hide. I was seriously alarmed about how I could cope with this complete lack of privacy, but was consoled by Alison's sublimely relaxed attitude. She was a little younger than me and can't have relished giving up half her room for some stranger, but she happily set about helping me unpack. She knew I must be tired after the flight and so, after taking command of the supplies I'd brought – safety pins, scabies- and lice-lotions, those flaming nappies – and showing me how to deal with the mosquito net, she left me alone. Fixing the net was a rather Heath Robinson business involving the door frame, nails in the wall and contraptions around the window. I soon learned that on hot nights you'd have to do a deal with yourself. In rooms like this, without air conditioning, you could sweat with the net or risk a cooler night whacking away at the little blighters, some of which always managed to get through the fine grilles across the windows. Either way, you got a rotten night's sleep.

An American called Nicholas was running the project but he had some tropical bug and was unwell, so I didn't meet him that night. Alison and I talked until I was drooping with fatigue. The next few days passed in a bewildering muddle of getting to know the people working there, meeting Nicholas when he was better and learning the labyrinthine geography of the place. I learned about admission procedure for the children and about how the rent and bills were paid. A daily routine was quickly established. Awake by five-thirty, when the toddlers had their first wash and feed (unless it had been my night to be on call to check wards and deal with emergencies in which case there was a short lie-in). At six the night ayahs went off-duty and it was our uncomfortable chore to give each of them a quick body search, like the ones you get at an airport. A lot of small things used to go missing and we couldn't afford to lose them. The women seemed to mind this indignity far less than we did and made quite a joke of it. Some of them were shameless about pinching whatever they thought they could get away with and displayed neither contrition nor anger if they were caught with something tucked into their sari.

There were about two hundred and fifty children at the home, ranging from premature babies to teenagers, with the number growing all the time. There were two large bathrooms and a small one for us and a total of sixty staff, including three volunteers. We had to do what we could for the children and simultaneously 'police' the ayah auxiliary staff. These women were on the whole good-hearted and willing but they lacked motivation. Unless somebody kept an eye on them, they would simply chatter, pilfer and pet the children if they cried. As soon as the night ayahs had left and the day ayahs arrived, we'd have some breakfast, usually toast and tea, while the children had their chapattis and wheat porridge, called sugi.

At eight there would be assembly and then school began. Alison, the nurse and myself, took the rare opportunity of the children standing still during assembly to give them the once over for physical problems.

While the older children were at their lessons and the babies being cared for by the ayahs, Alison and I caught up on paperwork. There were reports on each child to prepare for their FFC sponsors and general administration of the home. Nicholas was still too unwell to do more than advise from his bedroom. Benjamin, the cook, prepared lunch and we'd try and grab an hour's sleep in the heavy afternoon heat. The children, too, napped in the afternoon. It was a still, almost stagnant part of the day. In the late afternoon we played with the children until they had their supper at around six. There always seemed to be twenty little horrors pulling at my legs, twisting round my shoulders, clambering up my back to look for lice in my hair. This is a favourite pastime and once you've adjusted to the fact you get lice from time to time, can be quite relaxing. The children are smart and love playing games – a favourite being to sigh with horror, then to click their fingernails and pretend to have found a huge louse, then to run away giggling at the expression on your face. The children loved bright colours and usually wore incongruous donated T-shirts that might have been given by smart golf clubs and hotels and exotic holiday resorts.

Sometimes when I had a break away from being a human climbing frame, I'd go upstairs and sit carefully and tentatively, cuddling babies, gradually learning about their responses and watching how the ayahs calmed the fretful ones. Then there was usually a bit more paperwork, a shower if we were lucky or a wash with a bucketful of water if the plumbing was on the blink, a quiet, exhausted supper and another early night. I learned not to tuck the mosquito net in too carefully because chances were that I'd be called to deal with some nocturnal crisis and it was a terrible nuisance to fix the net all over again. Mainly I'd sit under my loosely draped net and read a novel until the book fell from my hand. I might not have slept much, always listening for a child crying or the drove of a pesky mosquito, but at least I rested.

It was much harder, tougher work than my earlier visits had led me to expect. Then I had no responsibilities and simply played with the children, took them for walks and helped the volunteers in small ways. As a crew member it was a holiday to come to the project. Now I was working there, it was like a holiday when BA crews visited and brought nice soap and other little luxuries – much as I had done when I was a visitor – and sometimes I visited them at the hotel and had long, delicious baths, a meal, a drink and a gossip.

Sandra Simpson, the founder of Families For Children, flew in from Canada to see how we were coping. Nicholas wasn't getting any better and was sent overseas for a break. This left Alison and me effectively in charge of the place. It was frightening, but we managed. I'd heard so much about Sandra and was really pretty awed. She seemed so competent, so confident, so familiar with everyone and with all the systems . . .. I was reassured by her presence but it made me feel dreadfully inadequate. She went around each room suggesting improvements, noticing everyone and everything. In the evenings we had long talks about what she had seen during the day, and what should be happening. Luckily she has a great sense of humour, which helped us all cope with the most difficult moments.

We'd been getting obscene phone calls and despite our measures to deter him, our mystery caller persisted. The police had been notified, we blew whistles down the phone, we hung up but he carried on calling. I took one of these calls in the small hours one morning – you couldn't take the phone off the hook in case the hospital rang about a sick child – and was so fed up that in desperation I began to match his obscenities, suggestion for lewd suggestion. I was just getting into my stride when Sandra walked into the office, wakened, too, by the telephone.

I could feel my face go scarlet and my throat dry as Sandra entered and clumsily tried to explain what I was doing and why. She calmly took the phone from my hand and began demanding that the caller offer to pay a fair price for her 'daughter'. She literally chatted him into submission. He never called again and Sandra and I have been friends ever since.

4

Families For Children

Sandra Simpson has twenty-two children. Four were born to her, and the others are adopted from all over the world. Many are handicapped or disturbed. The whole huge family – ages differing vastly, and some old enough to live independently now – has its roots in Toronto where Sandra and her husband, Lloyd, spend the winter, and in Quebec where they spend the summer months. Sandra's energy and emotional generosity seem to have no limits: there's always room for another child who needs care. She's a great inspiration and someone who could personally, immediately, confound those snide remarks sometimes levelled at people who are involved in charity work: in no way is her care for the children any sort of hobby or self-indulgence. Sandra is a highly attractive, glamorous even, woman somewhere in middle age, and has always been the driving force behind Families For Children.

After their work with Vietnam War orphans, FFC's work expanded and they set up further homes in Kampuchea (now again Cambodia), Somalia, India, Bangladesh and El Salvador. Although she will always fly to any of the bases and projects, Sandra works from home, more or less on the kitchen table. She's in touch by fax and phone with FFC offices twenty-four hours a day, and other stalwarts of the organization in Canada help from their homes in Montreal and Toronto.

Some time in the early 1980s Bangladesh changed its laws regarding international adoption. No one is quite sure why, but I think that a strong feeling that babies born into a Muslim culture should grow up in one had something to do with it. There were possibly some people who took advantage of the situation, but FFC has a very strict policy of not making money out of adoptions. Adoptees were only asked to pay a nominal fee of $1500, and FFC subsidized all the other costs involved in flying the child to its new home.

What the stopping of overseas adoption meant was that the home became steadily more crowded. In Bangladesh it was clear that there was a great need for in-country help, so they concentrated on that. At the time when the adoption law changed, currency restrictions were making any form of contact with the Western world difficult. BA had stopped flying to Dhaka because the business side of the trade had lessened so much, although there were still families to ferry to and fro. This very new nation needed time to take stock of itself and would do so in its own way. We, as visitors, would abide by their rules and work within their constrictions. The idea was to manufacture at home, import less, export less and thus stabilize the economy. The end result should generate more employment and national wealth, but it will take time before the policies and tactics pay off. In the meantime, the number of desperate mothers and babies can only grow larger. FFC nowadays mainly tries to give children a decent start in life and to send them off with some sort of professional skill and, above all, a bit of self-respect. The charity has always had to rely on the determination of its founders and volunteers, none of whom takes a salary from it.

The government and several major aid agencies run extensive programmes to promote the idea of birth control. Studies have shown success in this area is linked to literacy and other factors. No development programmes exist in isolation, and it takes time before the principles of programmes like family planning are understood and followed.

There are a number of pressures within the society that also have to be addressed. In the first place it is very important for a new bride to prove that she is fertile as quickly as possible after the marriage. Her status in this community is often perceived to be tied up with her efficiency as a homemaker and breeder. In many cases birth control won't even be considered until she's produced an heir, and that heir had better be a boy. Therefore she might go on bearing daughters galore until she finally produces a son – and then, perhaps, another one for luck. Then and only then will birth control be considered.

Without going into the social attitudes which allow this disdain for little girls to prevail, it becomes clear that, often, unless a woman strikes lucky first time she's likely to produce a number of children – too many to feed on a limited budget – and those children cannot expect the greatest emotional warmth or the best of care. The girls, after all, are disappointments. This may partly explain why there are twice as many girls as boys on our project. The necessary broad education in rural areas is beginning to happen. It needs roads, equipment, communications, buildings, nurses, doctors, teachers. The message takes time to get across, but progress is slowly being made.

Daughters are perceived to be expensive nuisances. They cost money to dress and feed, and then there's the inevitable dowry to consider if they have been matched to a suitable boy. It will take years of increased affluence, profound social change and enlightened thought and education before the situation changes. Our Bangladeshi staff occasionally help to arrange marriages if a girl wishes it and has no family to do it for her. There's no point in me making any judgements on this situation – we simply try to ensure that our older girls go to families where they will be respected and valued. We hope that all of them take some skill and earning ability to contribute to their marriage and new household, and with this some self-respect. This way the danger of them being deserted and becoming destitute is reduced. Actually (and I don't think this is very surprising), many of the older girls show little interest in marriage until they approach their late teens, if then. They've seen enough to know that early marriages don't always ensure a lifetime of comfort, let alone happiness. Most of our girls and boys delay any thoughts of marriage until they have trained in a skill that can bring them an income.

We must remember that an organization like FFC responds to the needs and cultural differences of the country it's working in. In Britain and Canada the vast majority of us live in the grey, neither in the bleak black nor dazzling white ends of the spectrum. In places like Bangladesh things are different. There are a few very comfortable people, and millions who simply attempt to survive. The middle ground scarcely exists. It's human nature to think firstly of one's immediate survival and that of one's family, and extending that concern to others won't happen until these personal priorities are met. We must all have a great hope and faith in the basic good nature of people everywhere – it's our only hope of a future on this planet. The women and children we work with are by instinct generous and sharing, but selfishness is understandable given the previous situation of most of the people we work to help. When people are destitute or desperate they can't be expected to think of others. Grab that food if you're hungry, or your baby is. Steal some more, even if you're full, because you never know when you'll see food again. It's understandable, but that doesn't make it any easier to deal with on a daily basis.

Within FFC we try to make sure you get what you give, sometimes more, and that grabbing and taking is not the way to make any community spin happily forward. But Bangladesh will need to develop and become able to care for all its own before the majority of its people can afford to see any sense in altruism. Stealing from store-rooms will always happen, quarrels over possessions are inevitable; but the hope must be that a notion of a common wealth will eventually take hold. With us no one is hungry and food is there every day, so stealing it must be part of some residual memory of insecurity and hunger. This will take years to blow away: it's unlikely you ever lose the impulse to grab and steal if you were deprived of basic necessities when you were young.

In Britain it is rare for people actually to starve: the food on the table may not always be very nice, but the food is at least there. The roof that keeps the rain out may leak, but at least it exists. It is difficult to explain the truly awful conditions that exist for many people if one's definition of being cold is the fact that the central heating has packed up, or of hunger if one has missed both break-fast and lunch.

On a personal level I don't want to mislead or give the impression that being close to such things improves your character. At least in my case it hasn't. I don't get any less cross now if I'm at home and the washing machine breaks down than I ever did. I keep hoping to become bet-ter-natured, but somehow it just doesn't happen!

The concept of FFC originated in a middle-class society with the luxury of trivial rules we often call man-ners. Whilst they are different in each household, area or country every child is brought up with an understanding of some basic rules, even if they sometimes choose to break them. If everyone in a society follows roughly the same rules things go much more smoothly. At home I've often wished we still had the system (older before younger, and so on) of who should go through a door first, as I perform a complicated 'After you' dance and then give up and barge forwards, probably to crash straight into the other person. The very notion of 'After you' is simply not understood, let alone observed, in the dodgem-car chaos of the streets of

Dhaka. It's every man for himself; only give way to something bigger and stronger than you. If there's a foul-up at an intersection every vehicle charges into the middle, usually blocking the whole thing so no one can get through. You all wait for ages, everyone honking horns, edging into every inch of forward space until a policeman finally arrives and untangles the mess. Patience and courtesy may be a luxury, but there are many situations where everyone would benefit if a little of both were shown.

The words 'middle class' are often used in a derogatory way. It's unfashionable, dreary and boring to be middle class and to hold those values. But I value the security my own upbringing gave, and think that the development of a large middle class is necessary before poorer countries can develop. This isn't saying we should impose our own values and I don't mean the sort of middle class I'm used to, but a strata of people who've received a basic education and are neither very rich nor very poor. From this strata rules and systems would develop. Whilst things can be very hard in the UK, most of us are never desperate enough to lose our belief in fair play, decency and sympathy for the unfortunate. Societies which have achieved a strong middle class seem to be able to extend these values elsewhere. I just don't see how fairness can be espoused in any society or culture, let alone voted for, fought for and paid for, unless there is a strong bedrock of people who have the undoubted luxury of voicing this need for their society's underclass.

It'll be several generations before Bangladesh develops its own version of a middle class, and it won't be until social desperation is the exception rather than the rule that there'll be much of an internal will to fight it. It'll never happen while people still need all their energies to fend for themselves and have none left over for other people. At FFC we don't get involved with national problems, but do what we can for a few women and children.

5

Raising The Roof

My three months as a volunteer stretched to five. The involvement with FFC had enriched my life far more than I could have anticipated, and I knew it had to continue. I resumed flying, pleased to be back in the swing, but retained as much contact with the home as my duties permitted. I took a lot of gentle teasing – being jokingly asked to sit on a towel so as not to contaminate someone's room, being called to the flight deck when we were over Rome to look down on the city where saints were canonized. I enjoyed all this much more than the earnest admiration that some people seemed to demonstrate – my discomfort at the latter led me to use the occasional extra swear word and to knock back lagers with a bit more ostentation than normal to bring back some feeling of balance. I also worked harder than ever on the aircraft, so that my involvement in Bangladesh should not be perceived as taking precedence over my British Airways commitments.

By now so many BA employees had visited and helped the home that an interest in the place had been generated in many of their offices round the world. I had the idea that perhaps there was sufficient British Airways staff interest in the project to undertake some serious fund-raising. I talked it over with my supportive boss, Gerry Devereux, who was then Cabin Crew Manager for the Tristar fleet and now works for the Prince's Trust. He'd allowed me to place a notice on the staff board which resulted in many colleagues bringing supplies to Dhaka. Later he'd visited the home in Dhaka himself, and was now very happy to help expand the interest within the airline.

With his encouragement I wrote tentatively to Lord King, Chairman of British Airways, explaining what we had been doing. He had already heard of the project and almost immediately made an appointment for Gerry and me to see him to talk about what we would like to do. My ambition at the time was to go round the canteens at the airport with displays to try and interest more BA people and to raise money. But Lord King thought we could do much better than that and arranged for Gerry and me to have a meeting with two directors, Howard Phelps and Ted Gosling.

At this meeting we went through lots of options. The feeling was that if we were going to fund-raise we should launch an ambitious appeal for something specific. That way we could have a target and keep everyone in touch with progress. We talked about all sorts of possibilities, but building a proper place for the children to live emerged streets ahead of the other ideas. The lease at Indira Road was running out, and there was a need to move out of the city. Less children were being abandoned and more destitute mothers were coming with their children. Often these women were deserted by their husbands, had lost their homes, and migrated to the city in search of work. Word of our organization travelled on the grapevines in the slums and the women found the way to our door. We felt that the destitute women should be trained so that eventually they could move on with their children. The more children we welcomed, the more help we needed to care for them. It seemed totally logical, to extend our help to their mothers, train them as ayahs and simultaneously help to preserve the idea of the family.

Also, children were staying with us until they were sixteen or so and whilst this gave an opportunity to teach them skills that would furnish them with careers it did mean that the 'turnover' was slower and we had less and less room for tiny new arrivals.

Indira Road was getting more and more crowded and it was becoming increasingly difficult to keep clean. Ask anyone in England about the smell that steeps the air in an infants' school and they'll usually come up with a description of something like the heady blend of warm milk and pee. I'm afraid that, since Indira Road was hotter and more crowded, the odours were a good deal riper than this. It was funny to see the little ones perched on long rows of potties on their balcony like a serried rank of baby kings. It was possible to grow used to the combined stenches of poor drainage, infant vomit, adult bodies washed only when the water supply would allow and nostril-lacerating cooking smells. The only breeze from the street was laden with the stench of the city's fumes. We did our best, but Dhaka city and our old buildings were not pleasant places to draw breath.

I had an outline of what was needed and had a trip to Dhaka coming up, so I said I'd provide a breakdown of requirements and costs after I came back.

When I got home I called Sandra, who was very excited and told me to start looking at pieces of land. In Dhaka I met a local builder and we worked out a very rough plan and costing. I also put word out that we wanted to buy a piece of land of at least five acres. On my return to London, Gerry and I had another meeting with Howard Phelps and things really started to move. The plan was very rough. Could we possibly think in terms of a children's village, large enough to care for more kids and have such 'luxuries' as an isolation unit, properly organized facilities and plenty of space for play? And if so, how exactly should the BA involvement be structured?

Mr Phelps had arranged for Godfrey Crook, who

was in charge of British Airways' Property Services department, to be there and he had the practical knowledge we needed. Godfrey was confident that he could bring together people with the necessary construction expertise to build the project, and he and Mr Phelps said they'd come and visit as soon as we had a site.

In the meantime George Bell, head of Employee Relations, came on board to help start the fund-raising along with a PR expert called Ron Scobling. We worked out how various departments might contribute to the enterprise and that we'd have to set about raising about £300,000 for the work. This was in 1985 and it seemed to me an unimaginable sum – an impossible target even with all the professional expertise that had been magically assembled. George organized a fantastic fund-raising committee with representatives of almost every part of the airline, from senior managers to trade union representatives.

I can distinctly remember the first time we all got together. I was a bit overwhelmed at the speed with which things were moving and had far more reservations than everyone else about whether we could raise so much money. But George and his team were supremely confident and never had any doubts that we would make and exceed our target. Even so, I was very relieved as well as delighted when Lord King said that British Airways would give us one pound for every three we raised up to £300,000.

A promised £75,000 was a marvellous kick-start, and so the machine began to roll. One of the beauties of the scheme, and one reason why an international airline was ideally placed to become involved with this sort of project, was that people working in many different departments had valuable and relevant skills to offer. We could tap into help and advice and practical assistance from engineers, architects, surveyors, lawyers, publicists and contractors. British Airways gives its support to a number of charities, but I don't think there has ever been a project that had the potential to involve so many of its ten thousand flight crew and other employees worldwide. Lord King took a keen interest in developments at every stage, and heightened the profile of the enterprise by being enthusiastic about it and gathering support from all sorts of important and eminent men and women.

No pressure was put on anyone, especially employees of the airline, to become involved, and a lot of fund-raising was done in conjunction with people raising money for children in the UK. Many people gave their time and expertise for nothing, and many others got really stuck in to raising money. We decided that all the money we collected should go to actual bricks and mortar and that our administrative costs should be nil or minimal. I wrote an article which appeared in the airline's staff newspaper, and after that the rate of donations from BA offices all over the world escalated dramatically. It was beginning to look as if that target really was achievable. Gerry had allocated a small office at Heathrow to be our headquarters; and apart from me, flashing between Bangladesh and London, two flight pursers, who were flying staff but based at the airport at the time, ran what had become known as the Dhaka Orphanage Project.

We'd had some lucky breaks already, so public awareness of the orphanage existed. *Blue Peter* had sent a film crew, and in October 1984 Princess Anne had visited. She was in Bangladesh as Patron of Save the Children. I'd spent weeks composing a letter to her, and when Colonel Gibbs, her private secretary, came on a reconnaissance visit to Bangladesh he visited Indira Road. I was worried that the pretty basic level of the place would be off-putting and knew, anyway, that every minute is tightly allocated on these royal tours, so I wasn't too optimistic.

However, back in London a few weeks later I was delighted to hear that she would make a visit. Gerry managed to arrange for an entire crew who had helped at Indira Road to be working on the British Airways flight

41

that brought the royal party to Bangladesh.

When the Princess arrived she was given a tour and saw several off-duty members of her staff helping paint a mural. Even they'd been roped in by the BA crew. She accepted a soft drink that I'd brought off the plane while the children entertained her with some dances. The dancing seemed to go on rather a long time, but HRH was taking photographs and seemed in no hurry to leave. Sandra and I were so worried that we were delaying her that we kept asking if she was sure she wanted to see yet another dance. After about the third rerun of the question she asked if she was delaying us!

She was very knowledgable and pleasant, interested in the children and their problems. Her visit was a great treat for the children, who love stories about kings and queens – and here was a real princess. It also helped raise the public awareness of the project, as it was filmed by a team from *News at Ten*, which meant we weren't starting from scratch when the major fund-raising started.

For me the business of fund-raising has always been the most difficult part of the entire project, much harder than running the village. I know we could have done nothing without the money that was raised, and believe me I'm grateful to every single person who contributed from the pensioners with their fifty pences to BA with their thousands of pounds, as well as the anonymous donors and the participants in and organizers of fêtes and sponsored swims. But the 'front of house' role and tin-rattling has never been my forte, and I was always relieved when other people took it on.

An old friend and BA colleague, Andrea Bennett, knew how little I cared for public appearances and simply suggested one day that she should take on some of the speech-making at fund-raising do's. I felt so relieved. I never felt I was giving it my best shot, and Andrea is much better than me at the business of speaking inspirationally. She also actually enjoys these functions. Over the years she's given hundreds of talks to schools, women's groups, Rotary clubs and so forth, mainly in London, and she certainly has the knack of charming generosity out of her audiences.

My two colleagues in the little office at Heathrow were Airdrie Terenghi and Maura McDonagh. Maura was fighting a twelve-year battle with cancer but threw more commitment and energy into the fund-raising than anybody else. Sadly, she has since died – but not before she had seen the opening of the village she had done so much to create. We subsequently arranged for a scholarship to be endowed at Sreepur, in her name, for the most outstanding of our thirty Catholic children to go on to a boarding school. Airdrie has worked for BA for twenty-one years and is now a Fleet Director, in charge of personnel and the welfare of cabin crew on some of the long-haul routes.

After a while I was taken off flying duties and the three of us worked long hours in that small office, meticulously logging and acknowledging every single donation, dealing with enquiries from the media – and getting on each other's nerves briefly at times! As well as making such a magnificent financial contribution, BA let us have the office, its facilities, stationery and all overheads completely free of charge.

Although British Airways was no longer officially involved once the village was opened and the keys handed over to Families For Children, Andrea remains tireless in her spare-time efforts and deals with the considerable volume of correspondence that still arrives at Heathrow. In addition many staff, including Lord King, retain an interest in the project. When our efforts were at their height I would often get a message that Lord King would like to hear how things were going.

Once I had the great excitement of being invited to a dinner at Number Ten. On the way the minicab driver was delighted to hear that I had a pass, which meant he could actually drive into Downing Street. He insisted in stopping before we got there and taking his aerial down and putting on a hat so that I would arrive in style. Lord King was also at the dinner, and invited me back with Lady King and himself for a drink at their London home. His chauffeur then took me back to Chiswick. I'd been so nervous that I had had a few drinks, and on the way I asked the driver if he thought Lord King would mind if I made a call on the car telephone. He reckoned it would be all right, so I phoned my parents to say: 'I'm just calling from Lord King's limousine to see how you are' in my best smart voice – then spoiled the effect by laughing!

BA's involvement has brought the airline favourable publicity, but I strongly believe that enlightened self-interest as a power to get things done is one of the most constructive guiding forces anywhere in the world; and even having said that, many large organizations would have lost patience with a project like this. I have both gratitude and respect for the way BA and their staff plunged into the Sreepur project.

Many of the great Victorian philanthropists – from Robert Owen with his model village near London and whoever it was who built Port Sunlight near Liverpool, to the great Quaker chocolate barons, Fry and Cadbury – managed to establish housing and working conditions for their employees which at the time contributed towards greater efficiency and thus raised profits. Everyone benefited, and that has to be the best way forward.

A producer called Desmond Wilcox read an article about our campaign in the *Observer* and contacted me via British Airways. He ended up making three documentaries about us for his series *The Visit*, and there was invariably an extra-huge amount of mail after each one. But I felt uneasy about having to live up to the image of the person I appeared to be in those programmes. I worried that if people discovered the less pleasant aspects of my personality they wouldn't help the children.

We received many touching personal letters and donations from people who couldn't really afford to give, like pensioners and children. One lady sent anonymously each week a twenty pence coin taped to a card, with a fifteen-pence stamp on the envelope. She obviously didn't have much money, but we only knew her christian name and couldn't contact her to say 'Please send larger amounts of money less often to save yourself postage.' Other people, especially elderly people, had been so emotionally affected by the plight of the children that they were obviously giving money that they needed. If we were really concerned, we didn't bank the money until we had contacted them.

Of course I was delighted to see the cash rolling in, and it was largely thanks to the television programmes that we raised so much more than we'd set out to. This meant that we could set our sights higher where the project was concerned and move on from the idea of brick sheds with corrugated iron roofs to much more solid structures. Every time the total raised crept up by another significant amount we planned some new improvement to the specification – better, more hygienic floors, for instance, or there might be more money to spend on the kitchens.

The Bangladeshi community in Britain has been another wonderfully generous source of funds and help. Again, the TV programmes reached a lot of people. A particular enthusiast is Tommy Miah, a restaurateur in Edinburgh, who is responsible for massive fund-raising and continues to promote the idea of helping our village whenever and however he can. He wrote a cookbook with excellent recipes for Bengali cuisine (well over 90 per cent of 'Indian' restaurants in Britain are run by Bangladeshis) and all the royalties come to us. He has also held galas, and at the time of writing he's involved in an Indian subcontinent chef-of-the-year competition which will help to raise awareness of this cuisine and raise money both for our children and for sick children in Scotland.

After construction had started, we still had one of the accommodation units just pencilled on the plan. We knew that we would not have enough room without it, but just couldn't stretch the pennies far enough to cover its cost. We had put in an application to the British Overseas Development Administration and were keeping our fingers crossed. Just in time it came through, a grand total of £45,000 – enough to complete all the building needed for the complex to function as a whole. With British Airways and so many people having contributed it finally rounded things out to have such generous support from the government.

These days sponsorship is a vital source of income for us; the office through which all the paperwork and administration is handled is FFC's British HQ in Beckenham, which has been run for years, from long before I appeared, by Trisha Silvester. Our basic policy is to ask sponsors to commit £6 a month (only £4.50 if they do it by Deed of Covenant, as there is tax relief). This money goes to run the project in Sreepur, which releases donations from other parts of the world to finance the other FFC projects.

It's wonderful to have things so capably orchestrated by Trish in England. She's also a good friend and a great support, although she does ring me from time to time to say that if she gets one more letter telling her how wonderful I am she'll scream! Trisha, Sandra and I share a slightly odd sense of humour, which has helped keep us going through difficult times.

The children became a very real part of the lives of those who were involved with the project. The word went round BA offices all over the world and the cheques kept on coming – £2,000 from New Zealand, another big cheque from South America. Crews actually started to request the Dhaka run so that they could see the original home in Indira Road, meet the children and maybe fix a broken drain whilst they were there. This was extraordinary because, as I said earlier, Bangladesh had never been regarded as the most appealing of destinations.

Each flight there would have a few extra suitcases, taken as crew baggage. These would contain blankets and baby clothes, woollies and nappies that had been given to us or that some BA crew member's mum had collected and managed to get to Tristar House at Heathrow for onward transmission. A volunteer trip to Dhaka each Christmas was over-subscribed. We took things out to contribute to the Christmas party we have for the children each year.

British Airways employs about 52,000 people worldwide, 10,000 of whom are flight crew. An amazingly large percentage of those people make a real contribution to other charitable ventures as well as ours. Dreamflight and Operation Happy Child both raise money to take disabled or disadvantaged children to places like Disneyland. Staff donate money – sometimes by direct debit from their salaries – and give their time without any great song or dance. It's not regarded as anything special. What I'm trying to say is that the idea of help and service, beyond that of serving lunch on a Tristar, is taken for granted by BA staff. What I got swept into could have happened to many others amongst them, and the work I do requires more commitment and hard work than remarkable human qualities.

I'm sure that many, if not most, charities find that after the push of some particular appeal it is hard to sustain the cashflow level required to continue working long after the reason for that appeal has been eclipsed in the public's mind by some other campaign or disaster fund. That's why the sustained involvement of people like Tommy, BA staff and the sponsors is so important. At the moment sponsors in Britain pledge just enough to keep us going on a very tight shoestring, but we hope to broaden our resources. For only that way – and this is a little ironic

– can we develop programmes at the village which will lead us nearer to self-sufficiency, so that we can eventually make products that will bring us an income.

I'd talked about the project to TV news teams, to magazines and newspapers. I'd been on TV shows from *Blue Peter* to *What's My Line* to *Wogan*. Every one of these appearances, often arranged by Airdrie who was wonderful at press relations, generated more money for the project – but it was a bit of a strain for me and I was feeling torn and tired. My relationship with Peter had collapsed as a result some time before, and I had very little left to give anybody at the end of the day. When I did have personal time it was so treasured that I often spoiled it by over-reacting if the smallest thing went wrong. From being relatively placid and good-natured I became irritable and easily lost my temper. Never at work – always at home. I caught any stomach bug going, and there are quite a few in Bangladesh; I lost weight, and was admitted to the Hospital for Tropical Diseases a couple of times.

All in all the fund-raising, project-organizing years, from the mid- to the late eighties, were exciting but stressful ones for me. It's only right to say that I got an enormous amount of support during this time from my cabin crew colleagues, who were always concerned when I was looking ill or tired. I doubt if all those colleagues realize how much their support helped me get through some very difficult times.

6

Building Work

Finding the land for our new home was a wearying experience. We needed a certain acreage, and we wanted ground that was high by Bangladeshi standards so as to minimize potential flood damage. At the same time the land had to be as flat as possible to avoid the nuisance and expense of heavy-duty levelling. We wanted to be within striking distance of Dhaka and near a main road and with enough land to grow some crops.

At this time I was still flying with BA, so even finding the time to look for land was a struggle. I looked at several sites but nothing seemed quite right or if it looked suitable we couldn't afford it. Finally I found a place about thirty miles from Dhaka in an area called Savar. It was a beautiful piece of fertile land, and I was confident enough to ask Godfrey Crook and Howard Phelps to come all the way from London to look at it. The day before, I checked that everything was going ahead with the site deal, and then arranged for us to make an official visit.

The two men, tired from a long flight, and me, feeling nervous – I was, after all, still a very junior member of BA staff – drove out, the last few miles along a bumpy dirt track, only to find that overnight a 'Sold' sign had been erected. Property laws in Bangladesh are complicated, but I had been told the place was ours if we could move fast – hence the VIP visit. As often happens, the piece of land belonged to a number of brothers and sisters. We'd been dealing with the brother who supposedly had power of attorney, but one of the others had pulled a fast one and somehow negotiated a deal to build a steel mill.

Both our visitors were very good about it, but time was moving on and the search had to shift into top gear. I was also aware of rumblings and grumblings about the move in Indira Road. The little ones were too young to take much in, but the older children suddenly acquired a deep attachment to Dhaka and wanted to stay in the city. Their unease about the countryside was compounded by the ayahs, who swopped gossip about murders and hauntings and frightened the children with their tales.

All I could do was carry on searching. In spite of a short extension of the lease, the time by which we had to vacate Indira Road was looming closer. Soon I found another hopeful site, but we discovered that it was totally under water during the monsoon. Yet another had a river of waste from a pharmaceutical company running past it.

A friend of a friend finally took me to see the site at Sreepur. It met most of our requirements and we could just about afford it. A patron in the UK donated the £20,000 needed to buy it. It was a larger site than we had thought of buying, but it's hard now to imagine how we could have managed with anything smaller. It was clear that there would be room for everything we needed from dormitories and classrooms to workshops and stores, from staff quarters and an administration block to kitchens and a refectory. It also only had one owner, which was a pretty positive point after the way the previous people had behaved. Best of all, there was masses of space round about for playing and for planting fruit trees and vegetable crops and to raise the cows we intended to graze. There were already trees on the site and it was plain that the soil was of a good quality – a deep, rich red.

A three-mile dirt track ran to the site from a small village on the main road from Dhaka. This was going to cause problems, but we hadn't seen a single place we could afford that wasn't stuck down a dirt road. This track has since been tarmaced, but in the early days it was rough and pot-holed. Several times during the monsoon we had to hire an ox cart to get up to the site. This form of transport might look lovely and rural, but it's very uncomfortable and the drivers are less than kind to the oxen.

Without going into all the excruciating details, negotiations for this patch of land too were set about with all sorts of complications and took about a year to complete. As soon as the land was legally ours our Australian volunteer, Mark Gillespie, went out to live there, firstly sleeping in a truck and later in a shed he constructed. It was important for us to have a presence there as boundaries in Bangladesh have a habit of moving inwards if someone is not *in situ* to protect them.

Godfrey had contacted a firm of architects he knew, and a senior partner there Dicken Adams, arranged to lend us, free of charge, an architect called John Lowry. John was absolutely perfect for this job, which I know he enjoyed, as his father had been a tea planter in Assam and he had an affinity with the area. He discovered that the word 'bungalow' derives from Bengali, and so it seemed utterly appropriate that the project (particularly since we had so much more space than we'd at first anticipated), should be a network of one-storey structures connected by verandas to keep people dry during the rainy season. The emphasis was on a solid, low maintenance, no-frills structure.

John became very skilled at balancing advice and choosing the most practical way forward. For instance, he resisted pressure to plaster the outside walls and instead left exposed the rich red-brown bricks that are made locally. The bricks are not only easier to look after, but they look better. He consulted local architects and contractors, accepting some of their suggestions but rejecting others. Within our budget – even though this was so much more than we had originally expected – he wanted to design a place that was literally safe and sound but not one which resembled an army camp or a Victorian public school.

Godfrey and his team of experts approved the plans and the building work began. Where possible, local materials were used; but quality was the prime concern and if necessary materials were imported. We used local labour and John came out frequently to oversee progress and liaise with our wonderful local contractor, Mr K.Z. Islam. His company's bid was put in at cost price because he wanted to help the project. Mr Islam donated all sorts of extra bits and pieces during construction and has subsequently underwritten the entire cost of our mosque, which must be one of the most beautiful rural churches in the entire country. It has the simplicity and serenity that characterizes many exceptional churches and will be an important place for the Muslim majority of our children and staff.

The building work was completed in about ten months. Given the scale of the project, this really is astonishing. All credit must be given to Azmat, the site overseer, and his suppliers and manufacturers – as well as, above all, the men we hired to do the work.

The actual building process was incredible. There were over a thousand labourers and skilled craftsmen on site and they worked from early morning until dusk. There was a bizarre mixture of modern technology and centuries-old traditions. Concrete would be produced from a modern mixer, then carried by a stream of labourers with baskets on their heads to wherever it would be used. The scaffolding was made of flexible bamboo which looked terrifying but I'm told was safe. I've even seen it used on skyscrapers but that doesn't bear thinking about. Instead of digging apparatus, another line of men with strange looking hoe-like diggers excavated the entire foundations. The site always looked chaotic, but it wasn't, everyone knew exactly what to do and where to go and there was not one serious accident during the entire operation. The most exciting day was when the specialist group of labourers were putting lime terracing on the roofs. The weather had to be carefully watched and when a dry spell was anticipated a lime-based mixture was spread on the concrete of each roof. This was then pounded with wooden batons for at least a day. The workers chanted and sang special songs and as they paraded up the bamboo ladders with their burdens in one long crocodile, they looked and sounded like something from a biblical movie. This traditional form of roofing was something that John discovered helps keep the buildings cool and watertight. It's often used in Bangladesh but rarely on this scale.

It was very exciting to see the buildings grow, to stand in the foundations of what would become my room, and especially to see the years of work and fund-raising turning into something real. Everything was accomplished to the highest specifications and standards, and John told me that had the work been done in England it would have taken far longer and cost about £5 million. All that waiting and planning had been worth it.

At every stage a committee of the building team and fund-raisers met to discuss the next stage. Lord King kept directly in touch via Sir Frank Kennedy, who also came to Bangladesh to see how things were going. We could call on expertise within the airline and outside, and it was gladly given. At contract stage we needed the help of BA lawyers. When we were worried about certain building supplies, there would be someone who would advise. We were able to get vital materials to the site because BA transport was offered. This all kept the overheads down and meant we could get the maximum value for the donors' money.

The male and female staff quarters are completely separate. We had some raised eyebrows about the fact that, as we only had one building, the administration block is not segregated; but we tried to explain that in

Western culture that is quite acceptable, even if it isn't in Bangladesh. John had the wonderful idea of an internal courtyard, and arranged around this space are the offices, kitchen, dining rooms, bathrooms and bedrooms. The courtyard is a wonderful, safe, calm, central square filled with sofas and tables and plants. Anyone who needs just to sit for a while or relax after dinner and look at the sky can enter this little oasis of peace. It's also the one dedicated child-free zone in the entire project. After a long and tiring day I might sit there for a few minutes, gather my energies and then walk outside where the children are playing before going to bed.

I love that time of day. The sunsets at Sreepur are spectacular, and the light behind a silhouette of banana trees and palms makes even our place look like an illustration from a beautiful children's book or an expensive holiday brochure. If it's the dry season I can now walk through mini-forests of verdant plants and trees, hampered by the gangs of kids who have followed me with their endless chatter. The little square of peace which John designed is a perfect refuge.

Because of the expert help we had I feel confident that we mostly did the right things. We accepted the best tender for the building work, and made the right decisions about design. The interconnecting rooms do not have walls stretching to the ceilings – there's a short gap which enables air to circulate. This was a design economy, but has turned out to be very efficient. The terrazzo floors with curved skirtings for easy cleaning, the sloping concrete roofs which drain water straight into storm gullies, the connecting passageways from veranda to veranda – little details like this, thoughtfully devised, have made real differences to the efficiency of the project.

I was wonderfully pleased with every aspect of the work as the village was being built, but didn't really understand how beautifully it had been planned and how cleverly Godfrey and his team had incorporated all our requirements until we'd lived there for a while. It is functionally very efficient, and as the years pass and the trees grow, it becomes more and more attractive. The buildings are weathering well and have proved to be adaptable to the extreme weather conditions, particularly torrential rain and strong wind storms. I have only the faintest knowledge of what architecture is supposed to be about, what the best architects strive to create and achieve, but I would say that Godfrey and John, Peter Wilkes, Peter Wells, Bill Foyle, and Dicken Adams and the teams that they chose to help them create our village have done a superb job. The buildings, their layout, the materials they chose and the ergonomic principles of the basic design have all been tested now, in the years since we moved in. Perhaps this is the highest praise that can be offered. It wasn't a perfect showhouse when we dragged our huge family up there, and for a few months it looked a real mess, but now it's a lovely home.

If you move into a new house you would expect it to take a little time before you learned that the morning light hit that corner of some room at a certain hour and so that spot is where you should place a chair or a plant. It might be a while before you realized that some room was where you preferred to sit by a window and work. The building team anticipated much of this sort of thing, but it was only after we had moved in that we could tinker and get things working in the way that suited. Their efforts made that settling-in process very much easier than it might have been in the hands of less intelligent and sensitive specialists.

Although every day brings minor crises with faulty electrics or blocked drains, these things are usually fixed easily. The hub and heart of the place has grown to be generally accepted and liked (stories of ghosts and bandits seldom trouble us now), and for this the work of all concerned, particularly those BA people and services who worked hard and fast to make it happen, can never be adequately thanked. Nor can the local craftsmen we employed, the people who raised and gave money to make it all possible, or the staff and children, actually, for whom the move to Sreepur was one-tenth adventure and nine-tenths fear.

Although it was a nightmare at first, the ultimately positive spirit of the ayahs and children has made the place work. We rely on that to keep us moving forwards. It's good now to hear them talk about their home with pride.

7

A Visit to The President's Wife

Once we'd bought the land, an underlying theme for the next few years was to get a proper road built up to the site. Even before we started building the project I was badgering the authorities about getting some help. The only trouble was that there was so much else going on and so many problems to sort out that I hadn't had the persistence or time needed to get anything done.

One typically humid and cross morning I was dealing with some playground crisis when Claire Taunton, our administrator rushed out to tell me that the office of Bangladesh's First Lady was on the phone. The bunch of little ruffians, whom I had been chastising for fighting their way up the slide instead of coming down it, looked relieved. They clearly figured that whatever was causing me to rush to our crackling telephone would make me forget their crimes. I tried to fix them with a 'don't think you've heard the last of this' glare and ran in to take the call.

A friend, Mr W.A.K. Panni, had recently arranged for the wife of the president, Her Excellency Begum Ershad, to perform the turf cutting ceremony which formally started our actual building of the village. Now he had asked her to see us in the hope we could persuade her to use her influence to get the road built. She had found a space in her diary but it was in half an hour's time. Claire and I exchanged panic stricken glances. We were flustered, hot and grubby and the water supply was on the blink. There was only half a bucket for us to share and we had to get cleaned up and dressed up in about ten minutes to allow time to get to the residence. I was very grateful Claire had agreed to come with me as I'm hopelessly uncomfortable in formal situations. She wasn't too happy to be commandeered into this expedition but I needed her to help me out if I got tongue tied. With her usual good nature she'd grinned and agreed. Now we stared at each other in horror. What on earth were we going to wear?

At the same time I realized that our old Vauxhall had broken down and our driver and mechanic, Mr Das, was out. There wasn't time to get a baby taxi or rickshaw and anyway it probably wasn't quite the thing to roll up at the President's house in one of those. I called Mr Das's son, Ajite, and he went straight down to have a look at the car whilst I went to wash. Not only did he get it going by the time a marginally fresher Claire and I reappeared but he had given it a quick dust and polish and somehow managed to change into a clean shirt as well. We piled into the car and as we drove down the lane I noticed the price tag hanging from his collar and yanked it off.

In the rush we had no time to organize our thoughts or to plan what to say at the meeting so we had a quick conference as we bounced around in the car. We would make polite conversation, thank her for coming to cut the turf at Sreepur and try and slip references to the road in wherever possible. I seriously doubted my ability to take proper advantage of this opportunity but at least I would have Claire to back me up.

We had to go on to the guarded military cantonment to get to the Presidential residence. The army guards at the gate, unsurprisingly, queried the validity of our appointment. Calls were made on mobile phones and searching stares were directed at us and our dilapidated old car. The minutes ticked by until we were actually late and I was going spare. I tried everything from name dropping to pathos but the whole thing obviously seemed very unlikely to the sentries on duty. Eventually the senior officer got through to someone in authority; you could see him stiffen to attention as he listened to whoever was on the other end of the phone. We were gestured through to the other side of the gate. The message that Her Excellency was waiting had a remarkable effect and we didn't just get clearance but a military escort. Claire and I tried to look dignified as all traffic was swept off the road in front of us, and our motorbike escort, lights flashing and sirens sounding, raced us through the streets. Unfortunately the back seat of the car was rounded and had been patched with shiny plastic. We slipped and slid about on the shiny surface and dignity was hard to maintain. Giggling and slightly hysterical, Ajite's feather duster dancing through the air, we eventually arrived.

Having been escorted through the last part of the journey, saluted by soldiers and stared at by everyone else, in a way visiting heads of state in Rolls Royces might have expected, we tried to arrive looking calm and composed. The door had been jammed on my side of the car for months and it didn't help that an ornately uniformed member of the presidential guard pulled and pushed at it but failed to open it. Red in the face, I climbed out of the other side of the car into a formal and silent courtyard. We smoothed down our crushed clothes and tried to gracefully to accept another salute as we were shown through magnificently carved doors into the lobby of a lovely house. The thought that half an hour earlier I had been admonishing a team of little villains for naughtiness in the playground almost started me laughing again but I took a deep breath and managed to calm down. I reminded Claire to cover for me if I 'dried' and we looked at photographs of VIPs who had visited before – anything to distract ourselves from our nervousness.

We were shown into a beautiful reception room,

decorated in pale blue, with lovely rugs and chintz drapes. The old, carved chairs were upholstered in blue velvet and light sparkled from exquisite chandeliers. There were little tables with pretty lamps and we were shown to seats either side of one of them.

After what seemed like hours but was probably only a few minutes, Begum Ershad, cool and elegant in a beautiful silk sari, joined us. She asked about the project, and the conversation, although halting, did move along. However, Claire and I were too desperately nervous to contribute as much as we'd have liked to. I knew this was my opportunity to ask for her help but the words just didn't come. I've always hated making direct requests anyway and this time I hadn't had a chance to make any mental list of opening remarks or to plan any sort of approach to the subject of roads. Claire was just as tongue tied as I was and it was altogether a rather stilted audience.

I thanked her for her interest in our project, for performing the turf cutting ceremony and for seeing us.

She said how much our work was appreciated.

Then there was silence until I remembered that she had recently returned from an official visit to Africa. I asked her if she'd been on safari and a deeply irrelevant and trivial conversation about game parks ensued.

Another silence. I admired some flowers in the room and tried to move the conversation towards the totally unrelated subject of roads. I failed.

Another silence. This one was relieved by the arrival of tea, biscuits and fruit. The refreshment was all the more appreciated as a distraction and another source of light conversation. Another attempt to talk about the rutted old road faded into the ether and there was yet another long silence. Claire complimented Begum Ershad on her sari. The compliment was gracefully received. Silence.

Her Excellency remained calm and composed. Her very stillness made me feel all the more agitated. Frantically I looked around me willing the equally dumbstruck Claire to help me out.

The glittering light caught my eye. 'It must be very hard to keep the chandeliers clean,' I ventured lamely.

She looked fatigued. 'I do have help.'

The ordeal was at last drawing to a close. 'Had she noticed the very poor state of the road when she had come up to start the building programme?' I asked.

'Yes' she answered and again the conversation drifted away.

After a few more mutterings of mutual admiration the Begum pressed a button and guards entered the room to usher us gently out. She bid us a gracious farewell and we were escorted to our 'carriage'. I felt a mixture of relief that it was over and annoyance with Claire and myself for not having taken advantage of the opportunity.

The relief was greater than the irritation and before long we were laughing and I was worrying about how I was going to explain my failure to achieve anything to our colleagues. Luckily by the time we got back to Indira Road we had convinced ourselves that we had made progress towards getting the help we needed. I could now write thanking Begum Ershad for her interest in our project and explain how much easier it would be if we had a road. I'd have time to put things clearly and advance our case in an orderly way.

The morning culprits were dealt with, the Begum was thanked and her assistance was requested, although it eventually proved that she was not able to help and we had to ask the President himself. This was one of the first experiences I had of dealing with major officials and I learn a lot from it and the other occasions that followed. I can now cope much better with meetings that involve making a request for the charity.

This was not exactly a typical day but perhaps one that is emblematic of the contrasts and surprises that happen on a project like this and of how varied the challenges it offers can be.

8

The Move to Sreepur

Anyone who has ever house-hunted in England, particularly when there was any sort of pressure to find somewhere else, and anyone who has endured the horror of even a routine move, will understand why I do not look back with much pleasure on our departure from Indira Road and move to Sreepur. There are things that I can laugh about now, but I doubt if I was able to raise even a grim smile at the time. I felt massive relief when we eventually found our site and then when the building was completed, but everything leading up to the opening ceremony was fraught with anxiety and complications. Moving is said to come high up on the stress scale, just below bereavement and divorce, and that's for a fairly straightforward house move. Getting over six hundred of us out to Sreepur in relays was only one aspect of it all.

By 1987 about sixty children were living on the site and over a period of weeks the rest of us joined them. In the months before we left I'd moved the children into the groups that they would occupy in Sreepur. I had also let the old staff who weren't accompanying us go, and had brought the new staff in so that the children would become familiar with them whilst still living in a place they were used to. I hoped that would make everything less traumatic.

The move happened in stages, and each day we

washed and cleaned any belongings of the children who would be transferring the next day. We were going to get off to a clean start – all cockroaches and other insect life to stay behind. The British High Commission lent us their truck and, with our own truck, we took two convoys of crying, travel-sick children each day. We dosed everyone with a travel sickness pill but they didn't seem to work, and the vehicles were sloshing with vomit at the end of every trip.

We all camped in the building that had been specially built for the disabled children. The first two groups were excited older children, who then started getting things ready for the smaller children. There was a camp-type, everyone-lend-a-hand atmosphere. The troubles only started when the women and smaller children arrived.

The first night the women were there the night air rang with screams as people decided they had seen ghosts or were about to be murdered by bandits. One woman threw a hysterical fit and didn't calm down even when she had been given a tranquillizer by the nurse. We ended up fetching a local priest to exorcise the spirit she thought she was possessed by. And the next day we got an Islamic priest to bless the entire project, which helped to calm everyone. Although I understood the ayahs' fear of the countryside, I always knew that in time it would all work out.

Something that affected us all, but me in particular, was the insect life. Since the area into which we were moving had previously been completely arable, the place was swarming with them – sometimes attractive and innocuous, admittedly, but in such numbers that some days they would cover the wall like an exotic living wallpaper.

Despite this I was only hurt once, and that was when an insect crawled into my ear during the night. You got used to wiping them off the sheets and pillows, but some always came back. It was startling and frightening to wake up and feel this scratching, moving irritation inside my ear. I turned my head on its side and banged from the other side, but whatever it was didn't come out. I didn't want to disturb the nurses, who had quite enough to do, but in the end I had to and, with a great deal of tutting and concern, they eventually managed to get it out. I thought the problem was over, but unfortunately it wasn't.

A couple of days later my eardrum started swelling and itching. I had to see a doctor, who found some small, painful boils inside my ear. They cleared up with the medicine he gave me, but the intense itching persisted. Months later the ENT doctor who had come to check the children took a swab from my middle ear and discovered a deep-seated fungus infection. He warned me that I might be stuck with it for good, but luckily the anti-fungal ointment he prescribed did the trick.

Other insects, though annoying, were not so health-threatening. The only ones that were a real nuisance were the ants. Parades of them would march across walls and floors. Every time you traced one nest and got rid of it another seemed to start. Food was stored on high shelves, but nothing deterred them. The big ones didn't bite, but you couldn't put a spoonful of sugar in your tea without removing its living complement – even when you had carefully stood the sugar bowl in a bowl of water.

The small, stinging variety were the worst. Once I pulled back the covers to get into bed and found a whole swarming ants' nest with eggs. Benjamin, the cook, and I spent ages carrying my bedding outside and getting rid of as many of them as possible. I still shudder when I think that I might have climbed in and stuck my feet down right into them. Another nasty habit they had was hiding in your bath towel. When you grabbed it after a shower they would then sting you in very sensitive places! Fortunately, as the project went ahead we were able to deal with these pests and they are now only an occasional nuisance.

In Sreepur, as in most of Bangladesh, during the monsoon season the heat is intense and the humidity reaches almost 100 per cent. In fact, it is pretty bad even

outside the monsoon season. And we didn't have air conditioning – just fans in the rooms. The sheets get sodden at
night and nobody sleeps well. Your clothes are soaked
within minutes of putting them on, and throughout the
country people throw towels over the backs of their chairs.
You can always tell which is the most important person's
chair, because it is marked by the biggest, fattest towel!

Because there are so many fans kept permanently
on at a ferocious setting there is a huge market in paper-
weights in Bangladesh. Looking through a pile of papers
for a particular letter or bill can be a hilarious exercise as
everything goes flying off in all directions.

At the start of the monsoon season a large number
of snakes, many of them poisonous, are driven on to
higher ground as their low-lying homes get flooded.
During the settling-in process at Sreepur I had the brilliant
idea of rearing some mongooses – snakes' natural preda-
tors – and using them to keep the project snake-free. We
sent word out to the nearby villages and soon the first one
was brought – she was called Rumi and was an absolute
sweetheart.

The second one, however, seemed much more nervous in temperament and bit me very deeply on the finger.
Since she failed to calm down over the next few days I
took her down to Dhaka, where I was told there was an
outside chance she might have rabies. If so, she would be
dead in about ten days. Luckily the British High
Commission clinic had some of the new vaccine which can
be given in the arm, rather than more painfully in the
stomach, but you have to have six shots at £20 each. They
gave me one shot, and I took vaccine for the other five
away with me.

The mongoose seemed to improve and started eating, and I took off to India to visit the FFC project there.
Two days later I got a phone call from Dhaka: the mongoose had died of suspected rabies. I carried on with the
vaccination programme, and when I flew back to London

just had one more to take.

There I was besieged with messages on my telephone answering machine and was told to return urgently to Heathrow, where they gave me a massive dose of anti-rabies serum. Half of it had to be injected into the site of the bite – since that was my finger, even the doctor winced as the hypodermic went home.

I was lucky to have been treated so quickly and efficiently in both Dhaka and London. You certainly have to be careful – a couple of years ago a British expatriate died of rabies in Bangladesh.

So all in all those first weeks at the Sreepur project were rather grim for everyone. The work routines weren't structured, so vital helpers would disappear for hours at a time, and we had trouble with the water supply. It was the first time in their lives that the women had had access to freely flowing, pure water. Both they and the children often did not turn off taps and showers and also managed to break quite a few, which led to an overload of our drainage system. We were waiting for our stoves to be built and having to improvise with the cooking.

I don't remember sleeping at all. I became used to lying wide awake and jumping up every time I heard a child's cry. I often worried about being responsible for this move.

One of the most remarkable and rapid improvements was in the health of the children. The pure water supply which tested as cleaner than London drinking water; the healthy air and removal from the pollution of Dhaka; the fresh food bought from a government farm – all these things led at least to better health for everyone, even if nothing else was going right to start with.

We had a number of volunteers come for two months each, and they also chipped in and added lots of energy and specific expertise which greatly improved the whole. As we were laying down systems that would determine the future of the project we liaised carefully before making any decisions. If there was a big problem and I was out for some reason the litany was 'Wait till Pat Mummy gets in.' Of course, when Pat Mummy did get in she was besieged with requests and dramas that tested her patience and energies. I was also dealing with all the everyday problems of administering the project, which were probably twice as complicated as similar situations might be in England. Life was difficult and I can tell you that I went to bed feeling anything but calm and benign most nights.

I was also feeling a little insecure. I had by now left British Airways, so that I could put all my energies into the project. After fifteen years there were people I was going to miss, and after receiving a regular salary for so long launching out on my own felt a bit strange. I had to travel between Bangladesh and the UK quite a lot as we got things organized, and the warmth and support the crews gave me as I charged backwards and forwards helped immensely. So many of them seemed very proud of the project and what we'd all achieved. Their encouragement also took the edge off my problems in making the whole thing work. It's still great when I get on an aircraft and someone comes and asks me how things are going.

I don't take a salary and am often asked how I manage to pay the mortgage on my apartment in west London. The answer is that I have had the extreme good fortune to have had a British couple, Michael and Louise, who currently live in France, as benefactors. We met when Michael called the project's BA office many years ago. He had heard we were doing something overseas, and they were interested in doing something for children in the Middle East.

I flew to Germany, where they lived at that time, to discuss possibilities, a short journey which brought about great benefits. Not only have they donated a considerable sum of money towards the construction of our fish farm, but they have also supported me personally because they felt I'd work and function better if I had financial security. During difficult times it made an enormous amount of difference to be able to afford some treat or just to get away. Perhaps they realize, perhaps not, that my knowledge that the London bolt-hole was there, that when I was in England I could see friends and afford to go out to dinner, that I could drive down to Cornwall to see my parents, that I could catch up with news of old friends without worrying too much about the phone bill, increased the quality of my life no end.

More importantly, this security blanket has enabled me to concentrate on my work in the village with greater energy than would have been possible if I was fretting about the bank manager at home. I hope that the village has benefited from their generosity in an indirect but significant way. This arrangement has taken me through the crucial formative stages of the village to a time when I think it is right to move on. We've become good friends and they never ask for any thanks, but I think they know how very grateful I am for all they have done.

The problems at Sreepur took time to resolve – they'll probably never all be sorted out. The women and children had been uprooted from a place that many thought of as home – they'd lost one of the few certainties of their lives. But it was thrilling as each hitch and bureaucratic problem was overcome. For the children and ayahs the place was stark and frightening, and it took time for them to learn to enjoy the advantages of being in the country. Where I saw peace, space and serenity they saw huge, empty and frightening skies, an odd silence, new systems that had to be learned, and a bandit behind every bush. What few roots these young mothers had were in the messy familiarity of Dhaka, and it would take time for them to come to regard the village as their home rather than a place of exile.

I hadn't exactly got the appropriate training or

experience for setting up an entire village in the wilds of Bangladesh. It's crazy, if you think about it – no wonder it was a battle! Even though I consulted many other charities for advice and constantly head-hunted for good Bangladeshi managers, in the end I had to make most of the decisions. Apart from the integral problems there were a large number of different buildings and even more different activities.

Let me put the entire complex into perspective. You come in through the gate and pass along a drive with coconut palms planted along each side – long-term planning here: in about twenty years we'll make lots of money selling coconuts. They'll also form a beautiful pillared, shaded colonnade. On the left is a playing field, then the tube well pump house. After that is the boys' vocational training workshop, where courses in woodwork, welding and so on are held. All our maintenance is also run from here. On the right is the school which has a large room for women's vocational training, where we also make some of our own clothes. The next building on the right is a big one with murals on the walls, and here our sixteen disabled children have their accommodation and classrooms. Just past that building, but on the left, is the clinic with a ward, treatment room and isolation room.

On the right are the office and expatriate accommodation building with its secluded central courtyard that I have already described. After the laundry, again on the left, are the dining room and kitchen and then you are in the central courtyard: a huge open space with the water tower in the middle and the children's accommodation around the sides. If you walk around the outside of all these buildings you find a mosque at the front, jackfruit and mango trees, staff accommodation, a cow shed, fields laid to vegetables or trees and a fish farm two-thirds of an acre in size. Of course, that's what this is now, but in the beginning it was just scrubland. It was very hard work to make progress on so many different fronts and it's not surprising that we all got a bit strung out.

I drew strength from other people's optimism and confidence, and when I was in England I lost my sense of gloom in the chatter and laughter of friends who weren't so closely involved and could see things from a better perspective. The great upheaval had been largely funded by these people, who were detached enough to be interested but not obsessed.

Back in London I found that Trisha Silvester's charity workload had quadrupled, which must have been fun on top of bringing up four children and working full-time. She kept her sense of humour, though, and was miraculous at linking the British Airways involvement into Families For Children's objectives. She had become involved with FFC when she met Sandra in Canada. Through FFC she adopted her two daughters from Bangladesh, and when she moved back to England she started the British branch of the charity. She's an example of the sort of person who has too much to do but still manages to do more. She'd been really brilliant throughout all the stresses and ups and downs of the FFC/BA link-up. Knowing there was all that back-up gave us the energy to get on with making the project work.

We've mostly had great volunteers, helpers and visitors, though a few don't like the project or can't adjust to the culture change. By Western standards we still have a long way to go, and it's difficult to explain the progress we're making to people who aren't used to working in countries like this. They naturally see the place as it is and notice the faults that need to be corrected. They don't see the long-term gradual evolution that is constantly leading to improvement. Mostly people are wonderful, but I sometimes have to bite my lip when someone who has been with us a short time tells me how we should be running the project. It's invariably well meant, and I have often picked up useful hints, but on just the odd occasion it's difficult not to say that I know that almost everything needs improving but it all takes time. By time I don't mean at the rate things move in England, either – I mean a lot of time: Bangladeshi time.

For instance, a frequent suggestion is that we should allow the children to brighten up their rooms with drawings and pictures. We tried this in the early days. The result was that the rooms looked such a mess after a few days that the walls had to be repainted. It has taken two years to come up with a long-term way of providing display space and to find the time, staff, materials and money to do something durable. We are putting up permanent notice boards made of a locally available softboard, then painting them the same colour as the walls. The children will be able to display their artwork without damaging the paintwork. It's actually a small job which will brighten up the whole centre, but with the medical, nutrition, staffing and other basic problems we've had it's only now come to the top of the priority list.

Admissions are very difficult. Sometimes on the river bank, perhaps after visiting a relative of one of our children in some pitifully distressed family living in a tin shack, I'll read the home visit report on their neighbours prepared by Puspu, our office assistant. I can tell whether Mr Haque, the project director, and his admissions committee are likely to offer shelter to this mother and her children. Our space is limited and our main criterion is to admit only children at risk. Not the risk that almost all children here suffer, but the immediate and probable risk of serious illness or death. Often people are not quite destitute enough for us to be able to take them in. I might have to interrupt a pleading woman to say that it is not my decision. I feel hard as nails and pretty awful.

Then I may watch the boats, long, narrow and shallow, cutting through the water with their sloping, curved prows and pointed poops. The wood is dark and the sails are faded and patched. These boats, elegant as clippers or gondolas, have been made for centuries and symbolize something of the river culture that is so integral to Bangladesh. Their grace and elegance belies the sorry banks that they often have to pass between. Rivers are still the arterial roads of the country. Depending on the cargo, which could be anything from a whole haystack to a morning's catch of fish, they glide slowly through the dirty river or slice across it with jaunty speed. They look elegant and sometimes majestic, a reminder of the timeless beauty of this country.

9

Claire and Mark

So far I've made this sound like a one-woman show but of course it wasn't. The two people without whom the move could never have happened were Claire Taunton and Mark Gillespie.

Claire was a wonderful volunteer who became our administrator at Indira Road during the time when the village in Sreepur was being planned and constructed. She also came back to Bangladesh a few months after Sreepur was opened and spent a year with me helping get things organized. She's working in Romania now, as a professional team leader, having worked for FFC on and off for about five years. Before that she worked as a nanny in England – having, like me, been turned down by VSO.

She saw the second of the BBC documentaries about me and the children's home, rang our office at Heathrow and that was that, really. In fact Claire spoke to me when she first rang BA, which became a bit of a joke as it was at a time when I was fielding hundreds of calls a day and I couldn't remember talking to her. As she'd worked in the premature babies unit at St Thomas's Hospital in London, Claire was readily accepted under the volunteer scheme in the UK.

She joined us in September 1987, when the Sreepur project was still in its infancy. Mark had moved out there, living first in a truck and later in a tin shack. It was extraordinary how self-sufficient Mark was – he was by himself at first, and didn't even take any books or a radio. He is one of the brightest people I have ever met, but he adjusted to rural Bengali life with no problem. He totally immersed himself in the culture and learned the language very quickly.

Having his authoritative presence on the site during those early days was invaluable in establishing our ownership of the land. The cliché in Britain that possession is nine-tenths of the law is even more forcibly true in Bangladesh. Even with his presence we had several battles over the exact boundary and one with the previous owner of the land who, months after the purchase had been completed, suddenly announced that the purchase price had not included the trees that grew on it. Mark was very clear that we weren't giving in to any extortion or implied threats. Being about twice the height of the average Bangladeshi male must have helped but his integration into and respect for the local culture was just as important. There was understandable resentment to our annexing of the land from people who had farmed there for generations and there were rumours that we really intended to build a church to convert them all to Christianity. All these worries were reduced by Mark's constant presence and even further when the first children moved up into a temporary shelter. The guardian of our wilderness was seen with a crowd of little ones scrabbling around his ankles and our imminent arrival to become part of their community was completely accepted.

Mark is hugely talented; he trained as an architect, and is now a highly successful musician in Australia where he has a recording contract. He has run a publishing company and written a book.

He is one of those eccentric loners you sometimes meet in life, and some odd quirk of his led him to take up the suggestion of a friend of his who worked at the British High Commission in Dhaka to seek us out.

Mark was brilliant during the move. As I rushed between Dhaka and Sreepur he stayed up there and helped everyone settle in. The first night we all moved into the expatriate quarters Mark wore jeans to dinner and smiled as he made the public announcement that his days of wearing the native costume, the *lungi*, were over! In the early days he was in charge of our marketing and food supplies and was wonderfully efficient, always determined to get the best value for every taka spent. He carried on developing the arable side of the project and planted orchards of bananas, papayas and other fruit trees as well as several acres of vegetables. He liked being with the children and they felt at ease with him.

Two things happened in rapid succession. One day I heard the news that Mark had been involved in an accident on the road whilst fetching food from one of the local markets. Around here, people are very volatile. If there's a road accident the drivers will roar away if possible. Otherwise they'll be stoned, whether it's their fault or not. Often if someone is hurt who has never been in a car but just seen them thundering past, villagers will set fire to the vehicle.

A baby taxi had pulled out and into the back of the truck Mark was driving. Mark immediately stopped to see if anyone had been hurt, and the usual mob that will materialize in Bangladesh, even on remote country roads, appeared. A nasty atmosphere, however, did start to build up: soon someone tried to set fire to the truck (even though the accident hadn't been Mark's fault) and a mob began threatening him. Fortunately another group of villagers restrained them.

A thirteen-year-old boy, who was a passenger in the baby taxi, had been killed and several other people injured. Mark tried to hail another baby taxi to get them to hospital, and stood by the body of the dead boy in a daze until the police arrived. Of course he felt terrible and, inevitably, responsible. Witnesses reiterated to the police that Mark had not caused the accident, and even the hysterical father of the dead boy agreed it wasn't Mark's fault. The baby taxi driver had hurtled on into the evening light without a care or a pause.

As there was a fatality, poor Mark was arrested and eventually released into our custody whilst the full investigation proceeded. We were told by members of staff that the thing to do was to offer the dead boy's father some compensation and pay medical bills for those who had been injured. The compensation went against the grain as we knew Mark wasn't the guilty party, but we bent to local custom. The medical care we would have offered even if this had been an accident in which we were not involved. Mark forced himself to visit the grieving parents, where he was embraced by both. It must be awfully difficult gracefully to accept forgiveness for a crime you did not commit.

But it still wasn't over. A few days later we met about a hundred of the most important and influential men in the area to discuss and resolve things their way. Poor Mark was by now whey-faced and shivering. He'd hardly slept since the accident. Although the locals absolved him of blame, they expected him to make things all right for the community. I was the only woman present during the confrontation with this frightening delegation. We were quite pointedly told that some gesture in the dead boy's name would be appreciated. I knew that the sub-text of this was that the local police would then drop any case against Mark. Mark started shivering again.

Mr Haque, our field director, was quite wonderful. He translated for us and made it quite clear that as a humanitarian organization we would be pleased to help with the medical expenses of those bystanders who had been injured, but that we would not be paying out because we accepted any responsibility. I guess this was one of the few occasions in their lives when they could see a situation in which their community could benefit from contact with, by their standards, very rich foreigners. For Mark's sake I wanted the whole business over and done with. We agreed to endow one of the new schoolrooms in the dead boy's name.

Once it became clear that we weren't going to give in to any further blackmail everything became quite friendly, and there have been no hard feelings with the locals since then. It was awful, though, to think that these villagers regarded us as fat cats to be milked for all we were worth. It's all forgotten and forgiven, but I'm afraid the whole story leaves a sour taste in my mouth when I tell it again. Let's just hope that nothing like that ever happens again.

Later Mark met a Bangladeshi girl who was working as a computer operator in Dhaka. He converted to Islam and her father consented to their marriage. Mark took her back to Australia and so we lost him. I do hope his marriage will succeed and I spoke to him just the other day. He still loves a challenge, and he is making noises about coming back – not to us but to the Chittagong area, where very few agencies work because of its isolation and the regular danger of cyclones. He would be in his element there and could contribute so much, as he did in the founding of our village at Sreepur.

Claire Taunton is very funny when she remembers her first impressions of Mark. He appeared to have gone native, greeting us dressed in nothing but a white *lungi* and looking almost messianic with his bare chest and long hair. We'd driven up to the site in the monsoon season and had had to struggle up the deep, rutted mud of the track. Being greeted by this immensely tall and eccentric figure was all in a day's work for me – but for Claire it must have seemed surreal.

When Claire first came out she was supposed to overlap with two rather more experienced volunteers, but they left sooner than we expected and so she and another volunteer, Helen, had to look after Indira Road by themselves. In some ways it was similar to my experience with Alison all those years before. Sandra, Ghislaine (Vice President of FFC) and I were due to arrive within about a fortnight, but until then Claire and Helen had to hold the fort with our local staff. I'm surprised she didn't do a runner, for this was also the period when we were at our most overcrowded. A British administrator who had been working there for some time had also left unexpectedly, so they really had to deal with a lot of responsibility.

The situation was unfortunate, but we did our best to cope. Our resources were very limited then, and whilst we knew we wanted to work towards a strong local administration there were all sorts of things that had to be organized and put in place first. Today the village is run with a professionalism that simply wasn't available to us in those days.

One of the advantages of my having a hotel room when I went in on trips was that Claire and the others could go along for a hot bath or just sit in the cool and quiet and write letters. I'd spoken to the hotel manager, who'd kindly given permission. With all the normal work involved in running the project and the Sreepur plans going on as well, Claire was working hard for incredibly long days. Writing to me later, she said that at first she felt as if she was being dangled by a rope over the snapping jaws of a crocodile.

Having survived that initial few months she proved so good we asked her to be our administrator which was probably one of the best decisions we ever made. Through all the ups and downs she was calm and good-natured, keeping the project running during the stresses of planning the move. She kept her sense of humour and always seemed to have the energy to be concerned about other people. By the time we'd moved to Sreepur she had returned to the UK but when we asked her to come back to help get the Sreepur project on its feet she had no hesitation in coming back. Mark and I were very relieved to see her and for a year she helped set up the new systems and management structure.

She remembers some awful moments when she first came back. We'd sometimes have to rush sick babies to Dhaka, and on one of those occasions there was a great deal of political unrest in the city. Cars were being stoned during a demonstration so she waved a white flag with a red cross out of the window and got through. By the time she got to the hospital the baby was desperately ill so she went straight to the front of the queue and grabbed the attention of a doctor. She probably succeeded because she was a foreigner, which is deplorable, but if you have a sick baby in your arms you'll do anything you can to get help fast. However, she was a very good organiser who helped get things running well enough so that such desperate drives are now very rarely necessary.

The children and staff still often ask about Claire and Mark and letters pass back and forth from Bangladesh to Romania and Australia. When they left us things had still not entirely settled down. I hope that they will both come back some day soon and see what their hard work has achieved.

10

Teething Troubles

Organizing the opening ceremony was a nightmare, but I hope we proferred proper respects to all our visitors. They represented most of the people who had been involved in the project: the British, Canadian and Australian High Commissioners, members of my family, some friends, and children who had come back having been adopted to Canada from the village in the days when adoption was still allowed. Security people accompanied some of the VIPs, and half the army seemed to come with the President.

It was all a bit of a strain. British Airways were very helpful in arranging for large numbers of hotel rooms in Dhaka for some of our guests, but by the time the opening ceremony took place I was on a sort of automatic pilot. In between drilling the children at rehearsals for their little show, spending the night before the ceremony helping to prepare food for our guests (food which, sadly, was left largely untouched because of a misunderstanding about where it had been prepared – luckily the kids gobbled it up!), I was fairly done in. I'd overseen the erection of a stage for the speeches, a decorative arch of trees, the flags and bunting, the canopy for the VIPs – and at the last minute I had to send someone searching for a replacement inaugural tree for the President's wife to plant as the original one had died.

John Emery, a BA manager who had been a staunch supporter for years and a particularly valued one in the months running up to our opening, was there. I had John to thank for the four-wheel-drive vehicle which BA were giving us as part of the hand-over process. We weren't officially supposed to have it until the ceremony itself, but John had swung things to allow us to use it during the build-up and it had been invaluable to have a reliable car like that while making all the preparations. The faithful old Vauxhall had broken down several times during each trip into Dhaka and it could no longer cope with the last three miles of dirt track that led from the main road to the project. We'd had to walk those, with whatever luggage we'd picked up in the city, until the four-wheel was available. Something like that piece of rule-bending made a real difference to the success of the day and probably saved my sanity.

In spite of my lack of experience in orchestrating such occasions and my great fear of somehow letting everyone down, it worked out. A symbolic key (which Godfrey had arranged to have made) was officially handed over by Lord King, on behalf of British Airways, to President Ershad, who then handed it to Sandra as President of Families For Children. It was a pretty symbolic moment for me, too, as I'd just arranged to leave BA and work full-time on the project from the end of March.

Mark, too, had his conflicts. He'd not really wanted to perform at the ceremony, but reluctantly (and brilliantly) he wrote a song for the children to sing, thanking everyone who had helped to make us 'One Big Family'. He played his guitar and sang it with the children. Later there was a party in Dhaka which I attended in a cheerfully sleep-walking way, well aware, already, that the achievement that was being celebrated was actually only the beginning of our real work.

The last of the VIP limos left in a swirl of red dust

and we were left with the debris of the great day to clear up. There's nothing like this operation to bring you back to reality after a celebration. This time, however, it wasn't like opening a window, emptying the ashtrays, washing a great stack of dishes, and sitting back with a last coffee and thinking to yourself: 'That went quite well, I think' as you might after a dinner party. It wasn't even the scale of the mess or the nature of it. In one way I felt as deflated as the spent balloons we collected and as strung out as the bunting we folded up. Mostly, though, I felt an enormous sense of relief that nothing had gone drastically wrong. The ceremony was a massive 'Thank you' to everyone who had helped build the village and it had happened with a certain amount of style and not, considering how complicated it had been for amateurs to organize, too many problems.

The sense of anti-climax must have been worse for the children. They loved pageantry and excitement – perhaps they had thought for a moment that life at Sreepur was going to be all treats and glamorous visitors. It must have been dreary for them to return to their chores and lessons in a strange place they weren't too sure about and in which systems and routines had yet to survive their teething troubles. The ayahs started their mumblings about bandits and ghosts again. Litter piled up and no-one did anything about it unless they were asked. The plumbing wasn't working properly, all the babies seemed to scream at night and little mutinies kept springing up. Everybody 'wanted' all the time – there is a word in Bengali, *Lagbay*, which means 'necessary' but in an 'I want' sense. All day long it was all I heard. For instance the ayahs wanted extra petticoats to go under the blue saris we supplied them with. I said they had enough. We started inexplicably running out of sheets (which are donated, incidentally, from the smart hotels in Dhaka, so they're old but of very good quality). It turned out that the ayahs were ripping them up to make petticoats. I read the

82

riot act and started a system to keep track of the linen so it couldn't happen again, but this is just one tiny example of the sort of thing that was happening all the time. As the set-up was still unstructured everyone was fighting to get the best and most for themselves. The whole thing was an uphill struggle.

Every time I turned my back, it seemed, another liberty was taken, another problem needed a solution. At first I tried to get everything working properly right away, but I soon realized that to keep my sanity I had to prioritize – teaching the women not to throw things down the toilet was more important, for instance, than stopping them taking extra food from the kitchen. So you deal with problem A until, perhaps months later, it's going all right without constant supervision; then you move on to problem B. That doesn't mean that you don't see and aren't upset by problem B every time you see it happening!

There were hundreds of things going wrong, all the time, which I had to juggle constantly so that the serious or dangerous things were dealt with first. At the same time I gradually had to introduce a sense of order. It got to the state where I did not even enjoy walking outside the office – every step showed me something else that really needed to be dealt with but just couldn't be. Everything seemed to happen at once and each particular problem seemed to reveal another, larger one. Several of the senior members of staff I had recruited before leaving Dhaka had not turned up. A whole management team had to be built up, which was slow going as most qualified people didn't want to work outside the capital city.

Because they saw they could get away with it, the ayahs were getting more and more militant. The ones who had come from Dhaka had worked a non-residential shift-type system and we then took no responsibility for their children. With the move we had decided to work on rehabilitating women with children and the ayahs' children lived on the project. They now decided they wanted the advantages of both systems without adapting to any of the requirements of living in our community.

Although we were paying them and educating as well as caring for their children, giving them clothing, soap, coconut oil for their hair and even a ration of the horrible betel nut they chewed, nothing seemed to please them. If they actually cared for their own child that child got all the attention and the others were ignored. So we had to make them work in different areas from those in which their own children stayed – although they obviously saw their children each day and, if they were breastfeeding, spent a lot of time with the baby. They resented the fact that one of them in each room had to be on duty to get up if a baby cried at night, so they just didn't do it. We started teaching them literacy and numeracy and basic skills so that eventually they might be able to support themselves and their families, but they just squabbled and argued all the time and often didn't turn up for their classes.

I started off by having meetings and being patient and receptive to their complaints, but I became increasingly cross and decided that, at that stage, getting the place organized had to be more important than having a democratic system. These women had spent their lives surviving by grabbing what they could, and learning that there was a point in planning for tomorrow would take time. Often I went to bed, picked up my science fiction novel (probably still open at page one) and thought, 'What the hell have I got myself into?'

I guess it's much the same as the feeling experienced by any parent lying awake at night and worrying about a difficult teenager. I hadn't expected anybody to thank me, but I hadn't expected them to hate me, either. One thing that made it all bearable was the resilience and warmth of the women and children. Once a new system they'd battled against was actually working, their

Held by my mother at Lostwithiel's Coronation celebrations in 1952

Taking wing with British Airways (*Woman's Own*)

One of our home visits: this tent provides shelter for four

A typical river scene in Bangladesh

With Sandra Simpson admitting a new baby at Indira Road from a young mother that can't cope (*Ian Spratt*)

A visit from Princess Anne

The new site at Sreepur (*Ian Spratt*)

With Claire and Mark

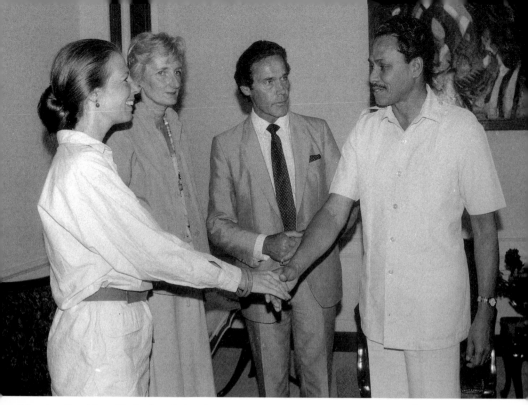

Meeting President Ershad with Sandra Simpson and Gerry Devereux (*Ian Spratt*)

The children's village under construction

Lord King and President Ershad at the opening ceremony of Sreepur Children's Village

One of the moments that makes it all worthwhile (*Ian Spratt*)

Mitu and Dulal in their new school uniforms

Monika holding my hand

Alal . . .

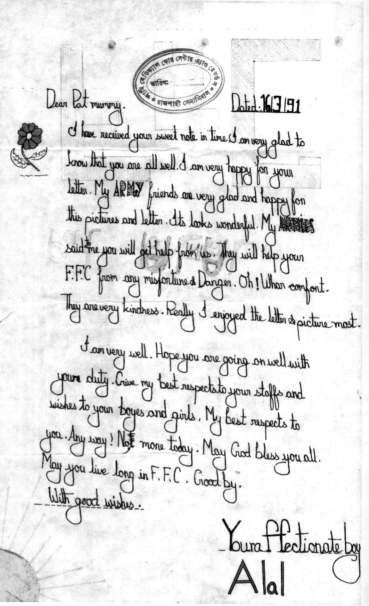

Dear Pat mummy,

Dated: 16|3|91

I have received your sweet note in time. I am very glad to know that you are all well. I am very happy for your letter. My ARMY friends are very glad and happy for this pictures and letter. Its looks wonderful. My said me you will get help from us. They will help your F.F.C from any misfortune & Danger. Oh! What comfort. They are very kindness. Really I enjoyed the letter & picture most.

I am very well. Hope you are going on well with your duty. Give my best respects to your staffs and wishes to your boyes and girls. My best respects to you. Any way! No more today. May God bless you all. May you live long in F.F.C. Good by.

With good wishes.

Your affectionate boy
Alal

. . . and his letter to me from the Army

Receiving the MBE in 1990 (*Express Newspapers*)

Wading in mud after the cyclone

Some of the children gathered in the village

(*overleaf*) One big family

grievances were soon forgotten. Someone could scream at you one moment and hug you the next.

Bickering still happens at every level. The ayahs in the kitchen may fight with those in the laundry. They may fight amongst themselves over something as trivial as how much seasoning should go into the food. Generally they rub along okay until something upsets their routines. I'm being very careful these days to uphold the authority of senior staff and to try and remember what is regarded as normal in this culture as opposed to mine. In an extreme situation, for example the slaughtering of a goat for the Eid festival, I will go along with the tradition but insist that it is done in some quiet corner, not as a public display.

For most of the senior staff their jobs on the project are well paid and quite prestigious stages in long-term careers. It's important to remember this. All are decent and professional people, but they are seldom driven by the kind of committed attitude that brings our volunteers over or leads people like Sandra to set up agencies like FFC in the first place. They also live in Bangladesh and have families and homes to consider, whilst we only come for a while. There are foreigners who are exceptions, like Valerie Taylor, and some wonderful priests and religious brothers and sisters who visit us from time to time, who can be said to have made a lifetime commitment. But they are a small minority.

Anyway, where the staff are concerned, personal ambitions can conflict and power bases shift just as they do in any office. The nature of our 'business' doesn't always come into it, although putting the children first is discussed all the time and the senior staff know that decisions are expected to be based on that principle.

There are occasional instances of not having filled in the right government form or having made mistakes in the paperwork. There is a bureau for non-government organizations like ours and, understandably, they like to keep in close touch with what's happening on the various projects. The government figure in charge of our entire district is called a Deputy Commissioner. Copies of our reports also go to his office, and his support is vital as he is virtually king of his District. We've worked hard at establishing a good relationship with the DC's office, and have been lucky that both officials who have held the post since we've been in Sreepur have been very helpful and positive. They have come to our sports days to present the prizes, and when there was a tornado locally the present DC thought highly enough of us to send the police to ask for our help.

A British theatre group, visiting Dhaka in the early days, came out to run a workshop for us and spent a day with the children, doing things like getting them to pretend to be various animals. The finale was to be groups of children enacting typical scenes from daily life. Great was my embarrassment when the first group centred around one little girl mimicking me telling the others off, coming out with phrases like 'Rules are rules', which I was obviously overusing. We had other visitors, and there was a moment's silence before we all started laughing and the junior actresses ran over and crowded around me, giggling at their own performances. There would also be surprising moments when a child would think I looked particularly harassed and would run over and say 'I like Sreepur.' Times like these made the problems seem worth overcoming.

I'm indebted to Claire, for in talking to her in the preparation of this book she reminded me, time after time, of things that I was too close to notice at the time – things like the improvement in the children's health, and how we discovered the nearby massive government farm which would harvest vegetables as we needed them. Buying in such bulk, we were also in a strong position to buy the best at toughly negotiated rates.

In all areas we slowly make progress. At the moment I'm looking at designs for a comparably 'primitive' type of washing machine, based on an eighteenth-century design in which a central barrel swings around and cleans the clothes without using electricity. The modern domestic machine actually operates on the same principle, and if we can establish these non-electric ones here in Sreepur we might even be able to begin manufacturing them in the workshop and selling them. That sort of enterprise is a good example of what I want to encourage on the project – helping us to become more self-sufficient, developing skills which the children can take elsewhere when they are old enough and, even occasionally, passing on ideas to other communities.

Our most tragic moments come when we try and help the child of a mother who was malnourished and sick throughout her pregnancy fight for life. When I was a volunteer we once had a very bad patch, losing four babies within a week.

Some women who come to us with children are also pregnant; we bring them in and have them checked by the doctor and put on a special diet. Our infant mortality rate at Sreepur is much lower than it used to be in Dhaka, which is probably not because fewer babies are dying but because the change of emphasis in our programme means that we see women whom we can help, and the higher-risk abandoned babies are taken to the babies' home in Dhaka or to other organizations. Making sure the mother is fit and that she breast-feeds her baby gives the child an enormously better chance of making it through that crucial first year.

If the children at Sreepur grow up to take fresh air for granted I'll be delighted: maybe they'll fight against Dhaka's blanket of smog when they're older. If they get used to the taste of clean, fresh water perhaps they'll protest about the polluted stuff that comes out of the standpipes in the city. At the very least I hope they'll question the sight of someone urinating in the river where someone else is brushing their teeth a few feet down the bank. I don't expect miracles, it's going to take years, but if our children learn to baulk at the conditions which are considered normal in most of Bangladesh's cities and villages then I reckon we will have done something useful.

11

A Life in A Day

Sometimes I'm asked about my typical day-to-day routine at Sreepur, and the only truthful answer is that there isn't one. Whatever I do, no day is completely predictable. I've worked in offices and in lots of jobs with a routine, but seem happiest when I'm not quite sure what each new day will bring. Exasperating as it is at times, I rejoice in the unpredictability of days at Sreepur: if I'd wanted a steady sort of job I'd never have applied to BA to begin with, far less got myself up to my neck in a project like this. Some days go quite smoothly, and that in itself is a minor miracle to be wondered at over supper. But most days bring one crisis after another – little ones like power failures and small epidemics of conjunctivitis, or larger ones like serious fights between ayahs and horrific accidents which require emergency medical help. Then there are the pleasant complications, like trying to arrange a job for one of the children.

I get very little sleep, as I find it difficult to wind down from the responsibilities and problems of the day. If I've flown in from England it takes me about two weeks to adjust to the time zone and sleep 'normally', as it's always unusually hectic at the project if I've been away. Anyone who has glumly addressed a post-holiday stack of accumulated paperwork will understand this. Even after I've caught up on the time change, the heat or mosquitos or a child crying can still make sleep difficult. I usually go to bed early, soon after supper, and try to relax with a book, preferably a science fiction novel. It takes hours to become engrossed enough in unreality for the day to stop spinning around in my head – always so many problems, all with inadequate solutions.

Most of the year, as I've said, it is hot and sticky, but the whirling propeller fans help a bit. They make a terrible racket, but this at least numbs some of the outside noise and they do move the air around. Wire mesh at the window keeps the mosquitos at bay. Ten years into the project and three at Sreepur I was given a splendid modern, quiet air conditioner, so future hot seasons will be less trying. . . .

Ten minutes after dropping off at last, it seems, I'm wakened by the combined noise of children happily screaming at each other in anticipation of breakfast, which is being noisily prepared in much-banged gigantic tin pots in the kitchen. It is about 5.30. These days, now that there are other people around to cope if there is an emergency, I can usually stay in my room all night. In the past I was so worried about nocturnal cries that I'd be up at least two or three times. No one could ever condone the violent behaviour of some sleep-starved parents towards their fretful and fractious children, but having experienced that kind of exhaustion I can begin to understand it. There were many times when keeping my temper was a real effort.

But now when the dawn chorus begins I reach for my ear plugs and crawl deeper down the bed. It's no use. I'll look at the wall and see the red smear that remains of the stray mosquito I managed to whack a few hours earlier. My itching shoulder proves that it had already done its worst. I lug myself out of bed and blearily force myself on to the exercise bike for my regulation ten miles. I freewheel mindlessly for most of my morning distance, hoping to do something about the slightly bloated stom-

ach that this vegetable and carbohydrate diet has produced. Then I'll shower – I do have my own en suite bathroom now – decide which of my unbearably glamorous
pairs of loose trousers and tee shirts I'll wear today, and
join the children outside for their morning assembly.

They'll have breakfasted by now on *sugi* – a sweet,
semolina-like porridge – for the very little ones and a
savoury wheat porridge with soya beans and vegetables
for the others. Just before school starts they sing their
national anthem and salute the flag, and seeing them in
their little uniforms, grinning and sneaking looks at each
other, always makes me feel touched and maybe a bit
proud. There are so many children of school age that we
divide them into two shifts. In the morning the younger
classes do academic work on the government curriculum
whilst the older children work in different parts of the centre or learn vocational skills. You can always tell when the
morning 'tiffin' time or the end of a session comes by the
noise as hundreds of giggling, chattering children rush
past the office. The kindergarten classes sit on mats on the
floor but the older children have proper desks that we
built in our workshop. In the afternoon they swop around
and the older children have their academic classes.

About eight I'll have breakfast in the staff dining
room with the volunteers, if they are around, and any other
visitors. There'll be fruit – mangos, pineapple or bananas, a
grapefruit-like fruit called jambura and, very occasionally,
lychees. One of the pleasures of living in Bangladesh is that
you look forward to the arrival of wonderful crops like
these – fresh from the plants, juicy and sweet. There's great
excitement as each fruit or vegetable comes into season. We
take it for granted in Britain that all kinds of fruit and vegetables are available year-round in the supermarkets, but
this availability makes them less special.

Then there'll be some of Benjamin's wonderful
bread and perhaps some jam or marmalade brought by a
thoughtful visitor from home, and a cup or two of Nescafé

with dried milk. Real milk is too precious and saved for the babies. A rare breakfast egg will be half the size of a standard English one and have a yolk as pale as a primrose: the hens here simply aren't well enough nourished to lay eggs with that blazing marigold-yellow yolk that we are used to at home. If Benjamin's away we make do with slightly stale spiced buns and tell ourselves that they are all the better for being yesterday's.

All this might have taken place on a good morning. In the rainy season there's no such thing. If you wash your hair on Thursday it might not be dry until Saturday. However often the towels are laundered, they always smell of mould. Damp gets everywhere. Shoes are clammy before you put them on, let alone after an hour or two – in fact most of the time the only practical footwear is plastic sandals.

Then to work, and another day begins – although the fatigue of the previous one often makes me feel worn out already. Maybe I'll give in to the wish for another cup of coffee: it's terribly expensive here, but it's a luxury we enjoy.

My office used to be quite a large, efficiently furnished room on one corner of the block. That room is still an office, but its occupant these days is Mr Haque, our Field Director, who is now in charge of the project. I've demoted myself to a desk in my bedroom. In earlier days my bedroom was something of a refuge for me, but now I keep the door open during the day and people know that they can interrupt me if they must. However, it's essential that the 'power' office is occupied by Mr Haque – it must be clear that he is in charge. I always try to make time when people come to my room to talk over a problem or ask advice, and I still attend meetings in the formal office; but I've handed over day-to-day control. I am now mostly involved in forward planning, liaising with funding agencies and occasionally oiling the wheels when there are problems.

Perhaps this morning there is a staff grievance to discuss. It could be something as trivial as one of the ayahs upsetting the rest by verbally or, more seriously, physically attacking another in the kitchens. It could be repeated thefts from the stores. We've tried to work out a proper procedure for such grievances and have visited other projects to see how they cope. We're working on the draft of a formal policy document. In the meantime we have to work with somewhat hysterical reactions to the slightest disruption or change – mass resignations, abusive reports to the central FFC office in Canada, tearful complaints and accusations.

On a quieter morning Mr Haque and I will discuss the programme for the day. A typical, minor problem could be that several members of staff want to attend a wedding in Dhaka later that week. As it's essential for everyone to realize that our cars are only to be used for project business – diesel fuel is expensive – we have a policy of not allowing a car to be used for a free ride like this. We agree a 'fare' for all those who want to go. I'm sure this sounds very petty, but the money we receive is all given to the children and we must spend it as carefully as possible. With eight hundred people living in Sreepur, the rules need to be very specific or things could quickly get out of control.

Recently, having asked the nurses to monitor the consumption of basic medicines on the project, we noticed that we were using 1200 tablets of paracetamol per month. The ayahs were all getting headaches, and as they tend to suffer from hypochondria they think they need a tablet or injection to cure the slightest pain. I'd never deny a painkiller to someone who was truly suffering, but some of the women were taking far too many without seeing a doctor. Large quantities of this sort of drug can damage the kidneys, and the expense was also very high. At one of our weekly staff meetings I suggested that we had a trial month where anyone requiring tablets either had to see a doctor and get a prescription or pay a nominal amount for a tablet. There was a good deal of grumbling, but the following month's consumption of paracetamol fell to less than twenty tablets.

If it's the day of the staff meeting again, Mr Haque is in the chair. Last week's minutes are discussed, and we try to ensure that action has been taken and track any longer-term issues. Each supervisor reports on their area of responsibility: what has been fixed, what still needs attention. It's a simple system and should work well enough, but at first when I went away the procedures and discipline on the project broke down. Several times I came back to absolute chaos. It was very, very depressing to see how quickly order can deteriorate in this way, and my biggest task has been to work with Mr Haque and his management team on systems and rules that can prevent this happening again. In the short term, an absolute dictator committed to making the project work is an effective way of bringing order to chaos. In the long term, a good management team and policies are essential.

When I'm not here there's a noticeable increase in litter about the place, the children forget some of their table manners, stand on desks in the classrooms, play in areas where they know they shouldn't. . . . Things are really looking up, but it will take a little more time. As it is, I still have to be a sort of policeman and take time every day to walk round each part of the village to make sure that things are up to scratch. It's an odd sensation – accepting all that touching affection from the children, 'Pat Mummy, Pat Mummy', and simultaneously being the ultimate source of discipline. The children and women often get really angry when we clamp down on something like not issuing new clothes unless we can see that the old ones are worn out or outgrown. However, I guess they know I'm basically on their side because the sulks seldom last long and I'm 'Pat Mummy' again.

A lot of the staff, particularly the less educated

ones, are quite happy to perform their prescribed duties and then switch off. So, for example, if a kitchen ayah has finished her work and walks past laundry that has fallen off the line and into the mud, she won't think to pick it up. That's not her job. We've tried all sorts of motivation schemes but nothing has worked yet. In discussion everyone seems to understand that this is their home and that it'll be a more comfortable one for everyone if we all help, but it will take a while before the principle of enlightened self-interest takes hold and we can rely on the staff and ayahs to widen their vision.

Sadly, the most successful solution in the past has been to have expatriates whose enthusiasm rubs off on to everyone else. For years the children and more junior staff have to defer to foreigners and trust them to do things fairly. Again, it will take time to effect a change in this attitude, to encourage self-motivation in our Bangladeshi staff and an understanding that taking a personal responsibility for even small things is better than hoping that someone else will get you out of a jam.

In a way this trust in the authority of a foreigner is emblematic of the way many Bangladeshis see themselves and their country. Poverty and frequent natural disasters have resulted in an unfortunate dependence upon foreign aid. Sometimes this deference, this lack of self-respect merely annoys me. At other times I despair. We teach the children the history of their country, about Dhaka muslin, which was the finest fabric in the world for two thousand years, and traditional dances and songs. We hope they will grow up with a positive, optimistic outlook.

At the staff meeting we discuss strengthening our management team again. Although expatriates have played a useful role, the future of Sreepur lies in the hands of the Bangladeshi management who can raise the children within the culture of their own country. It will be run even better than it is today.

We always decide on an annual motto, and for

1991 we put up signs saying: 'Prevention is Better than Cure'. We decided to keep that as our permanent maxim, and have a joke with a senior staff member who went out for the signs and returned with an extra four saying: 'Do not Spit Hither and Thither'. The language was old-fashioned, but the message was a good one!

We talk about all the systems we have in place and their success and sometimes failure. Stealing has been reduced as we have given each pair of ayahs a lockable cupboard and clothes, soap, a sewing kit, toys, tooth powder and so on so they can look after the children in their care.

A good example of our 'prevention is better than cure' policy which has worked was a campaign against ringworm, a fungus that causes a very itchy round area. Every night for more than a month we rounded up every single child with ringworm – over a hundred – and treated them. The children had always been given medication as cases came to light, but this time we examined every single child and even the mildest case was treated. For the first time ever we completely got rid of the fungus. Of course it's since been reintroduced, but we've been able to contain the new outbreaks. We've also virtually eliminated the nasty secondary infections the children would get, having scratched away at their itchy scabs. With fewer cases of infection the nurses' workload has also decreased, and all the staff are starting to see the advantage of this sort of planning.

Some days there are visitors – sometimes people from other aid projects, sometimes journalists, sometimes diplomats or their wives and families looking around to see how they might help us. Whenever possible I like to spend time with them and pray that they understand if things are a big chaotic. We are a very small charity and really need all the help that we can get. I'll show visitors our well, for example, and explain that by drilling so deep we have absolutely pure water – rare not just in

Bangladesh but worldwide. This alone makes a huge difference to the children's health. The mains water in Dhaka
has to be filtered and boiled, to avoid disease, so the
significance of this is easily appreciated. Pure water has to
be one of the most important things you can provide for
these children.

Visitors see the schoolrooms, workshop, store-
rooms, kitchen and laundry, and if the weather is fine
enough I'll show them our little farm. We have cows, a
wheat mill and beehives, as well as avocado, guava,
mango, plaintain, banana and papaya trees. We are even
cultivating cashew nuts. It really is very verdant and fruit-
ful and, although we cannot hope to be completely self-
sufficient, we aim to depend less and less on external
supplies. As yet the bulk of our food supplies still come
from the markets, but we now have a marketing officer
who checks prices and quality.

Some visitors, especially business people on a short
stay in Bangladesh, may think our children have a pretty
tough life, but only if they have never seen the destitution
that the children and their mothers endured before desperation led them to us. I know the project has a long way
to go and that it is, after all, an institution; but with more
and more emphasis on training the mothers, hopefully the
children will stay with us for shorter lengths of time. I
sometimes have too assure such visitors that the village is
like the Ritz compared to where the children were before.

When we move to see the children at play the visitors are invariably mobbed, the children excited, curious
and welcoming. They touch and clamour, chatter and tug
clothing. Some guests enjoy this, but others find it overwhelming. All the kids want their photographs taken and
most visitors are delighted to oblige.

A quick look into the relative peace of the baby
house, where the really tiny ones are cared for, and then
back inside the administration house for lunch. On the
way I explain that nothing on the project is wasted.

Everything is recycled in some way or another, whether it's plastic bottles for toys or fruit peelings for compost. We have special eco-stoves in the kitchens which greatly reduce our consumption of firewood. They look like great concrete hippos but have been expertly designed to consume little fuel and retain their heat, which in a country that needs to conserve its forests is important. It's only been two years since we had electricity connected – thanks to President Ershad and the government of Bangladesh – and that's helped enormously.

We visit the vocational training workshops where the children, who are also taught paramedic skills, learn weaving, embroidery, carpentry, mechanics, building and electrics. When they leave they are better equipped than most young people in the country to find work. In the meantime they help to service and maintain the equipment here at Sreepur.

Lunch invariably includes some soup prepared by Benjamin. My favourite is his sweet pumpkin served with fresh lentil-filled paratha. There'll be a salad if the right vegetables are in season, fresh fruit and perhaps some pineapple juice. Also on the table may be the remains of last night's supper and an odd collection of jars and bottles donated by earlier visitors – Marmite, Worcester sauce, some jam. We eat well but simply, and nothing is wasted.

Benjamin has been with FFC for over ten years now. He's scrupulous about cleanliness, so no one who eats with us need have any fear about getting sick. Our food is prepared separately from that of the children but it is essentially made from the same produce. We eat from an odd but fun collection of mismatched plates, glasses and cutlery, and I'm now slightly startled if my side plate matches the main one. As ever, I'm very concerned that money sent to the village goes towards the welfare of the children, not to the comforts of the staff. It's pleasant to eat off decent china in England, but it's really not a priority here (although we did buy a local set to use when VIPs came for the opening ceremony). Embassy staff or returning industrialists sometimes sell their household effects before leaving for home, and quite a few give us bits and pieces.

The visitors are very kind and sometimes invite me to functions in Dhaka. Puspu, our office assistant, who has also been with us since the early days in Indira Road, reminded me recently of an occasion when I was asked to a rather grand diplomatic function in Dhaka. I did not have anything suitable to wear so I asked her to search through the children's clothing store in case there was anything there that I could adapt. She found two or three frocks and we had a fashion parade, to everyone's amusement. One almost fitted and, with the help of our tailor and some gilt chains, the children thought it looked great – so Cinderella went to the ball! I wondered about what was going through the mind of the woman who despatched a discarded cocktail dress to a children's village in Bangladesh, but none the less I am very grateful to her.

After lunch – which the guests seem to enjoy – I've got another meeting with Mr Haque. The visitors gulp their coffee and return to Dhaka. We have more problems with departments failing to liaise properly, the marketing officer failing to get information soon enough to co-ordinate his trips to the various markets efficiently, an outbreak of conjunctivitis in the baby wing which may mean isolating some children to prevent it spreading. All these are dealt with and then put on the agenda of the next staff meeting for further group discussion.

And there's a more immediate problem: a boy has broken his arm playing football and needs to have an X-ray in Dhaka. As one of the trucks was leaving anyway, with the driver instructed to perform such errands as paying our electricity bill and buying some nails, I rush to find an ayah to accompany the boy to Dhaka and take care of him while he waits for treatment in hospital.

On my return to my room I glare at the stack of paperwork and try, at least, to make an inroad. There's a racket outside my window. Some child thinks he has been hard done by and chooses this particular spot to bawl. It's an old trick to stand outside my room and cry, but I'm too used to it to be very receptive. I have a quick look to make sure it's nothing serious, then I fetch the Centre Supervisor and ask for a bit of peace, and some of the paperwork eventually gets done.

At about six o'clock, when the bell rings for the first shift in the dining room, I drag myself over. Everyone knows that I am very strict on basic eating habits, so unfortunately my very presence there does a lot for manners and discipline. As word of my imminent arrival spreads there is no further jumping on benches, the noise level subsides and they sit like smiling little angels.

Later that evening there could be a power cut – extremely irritating if I still planned to work but pretty common, I'm afraid. It's not a disaster. Whilst we wait for the generator to be turned on there's a gas cylinder in the kitchen so Benjamin can still cook, and those of us who are around can eat our supper in unromantic candle-lit gloom and run through the events of the day. The generator is left on until 10.30 p.m., by which time the children are all in bed asleep and most of the day's work is done.

Some of these evenings are really fun, particularly if there are six or seven of us, volunteers and old friends, round the table. Sometimes it's just me and my novel. In any event, after supper I've usually had enough and head towards my room and the hope of sleep.

12

Time Out

The only time most people read, think or talk about Bangladesh is in time of crisis, which the country certainly has more than its fair share of. Few people are aware that it is a rather beautiful place but despite some rather half-hearted attempts, there is virtually no tourist trade which is probably a mixed blessing. Those parts of the landscape which are serenely and gently verdant remain unspoilt and, although sightings are rare indeed, Royal Bengal tigers do still roam the forests of the delta. Enchanting traditions are maintained in their purest form, not altered for tourist shows. Women still wear saris; in the cities some also wear the elegant and traditional shalwar chemise – a long tunic over baggy trousers which taper in at the ankle. Many men still wear the *lungi*, a long skirt knotted at the waist and falling in deep folds at the front. It is far cooler and more practical than trousers. A few teams of oxen still jostle for space in city streets as well as on the country roads and rutted tracks.

Far away from the city there are little markets at every intersection of roads but behind these centres of noisy commerce are great, largely flat expanses of forest and farmland and rice fields. Mud-hut villages hide and nestle within the shadows of the landscape, making it seem deceptively underpopulated. The climate swings dramatically but in the winter months it is warm during the day and cool in the evenings. These evenings can be especially pleasant. A deep violet light comes with the sunset, bathing the country areas with an almost fairy-tale, colouring-book prettiness and the cities with a sort of natural neon glamour. Bangladesh must show the world more of its natural beauty and that of its artisans and poets.

Even as it is, there is a side of life in Bangladesh, and particularly Dhaka, into which I dip and sometimes literally dive that is very different from the plain day-to-day life of Sreepur and which seems to exist whether or not the country is smitten by climactic or other disaster. Were Sreepur not such a long and petrol-consuming drive from the capital I would go there more often as this other aspect of life is restorative and enjoyable and my access to it is only restricted by distance.

There is a small British community in Dhaka – less than a thousand people – who lead a very different life from that of the indigenous population. There are the diplomats and their families, although it has to be said that some people regard a posting to Dhaka as the short straw and would very much rather be in Paris, Rome or Washington. Many are relieved when their tour of duty is over. Business people and airline staff pass through and usually stay at one or other of the five-star hotels. Some airline staff, of course, actually live in the city as do executives of the several pharmaceutical, banking, engineering and tea-growing companies. They tend to live, like the diplomats, in a pleasant, leafy area surprisingly close to the heart of the city. Some have cultivated the most fragrant and peaceful gardens, along English lines, but cultivating spectacular local flowers and shrubs. And then there is the aid community. Families For Children is very small but most of the major agencies such as Oxfam, Care and Save the Children have projects here. Not surprisingly, we do all tend to know one another or at least know of each other.

Dhaka is not a designed city like Paris, and its historical evolution has led to a number of different centres – the industrial, commercial, diplomatic, political and so on. Unlike most Western capitals, however, the character of an area can change abruptly and within seconds you can leave the bustle of a commercial district for the calm of a prosperous residential one. The word 'Dhaka' means within the sound of a drum and the original community spread as far as the reverberation could reach. The apparent chaos isn't without its own charm. Yards away from portentous modern parliamentary buildings on streets wide enough for grand parades are beauty parlours and shabby food stores with peeling jade- and lilac-coloured paintwork. The elegant gardens and fountains of international hotels and elaborate mosques abut the noisy squalor of street markets and slum dwellings made from corrugated iron. A grey pall of exhaust fumes clouds the city from a distance and assaults you on arrival. In the hot season we close the window of the car if we're driving in to the centre and give in to the luxury of its expensive-to-run air conditioning.

Londoners think their city is choked but the jams in Dhaka are almost comically worse. The garishly-decorated rickshaw taxis, the three-wheeled motorized ones, lean and tired boys on bicycles pulling carts loaded as high as haystacks, teams of oxen dragging farm produce all clog the streets. Western vehicles such as ours add to the mixture. It can take hours to cross the city so there's plenty of time to read mis-spelled advertising hoardings extolling the lure of expensive foreign goods like Seven-Up and Japanese cars. The advertisements will have their quirky English translation alongside the Bengali legend. The noise, the smells and the occasional shattered windscreen, if you're unlucky enough to be caught in the midst of one of the occasional street riots, are all overwhelming. And then, defying the odds in a city where no one appears to observe traffic regulations, you turn a corner into a

103

relatively peaceful area where the diplomats and industrial leaders and most of Bangladesh's super-rich live.

Sometimes I go to diplomatic functions in this area.
I have a few very smart things in the wardrobe at Sreepur
for such evenings, bought mainly from second-hand
designer shops in London. As I've already said I've also
borrowed from the children's store every now and then.
It's wonderful how someone else's elegant cast-offs can be
recycled. One reason why even very poor people in
Bangladesh usually look smart is that there is no inhibition
about buying second-hand clothes. There's no stigma at all
and new clothes are usually only bought for festivals.
Driving into Dhaka decked out in smart if not new
designer glory and wearing make-up (often applied by
using the car's side mirror as I'm always running late for
these do's) I do feel a bit strange. The occasion may be
purely social but there's always a sub-text of work beneath
the small talk. It often happens that I find myself talking to
someone who might be able to help the project in some
way. Lots of useful connections are made at these functions and I'm more than happy to dress-up and make-up.
The chatting bit is sometimes difficult as my life is so odd.
It's sometimes hard to find something to say that doesn't
involve droning on about Sreepur. I have to rack my mind
desperately for some appropriate light conversation.

Bangladesh is a Muslim country so liquor is only
available in private homes or, expensively, in hotel bars.
At this kind of dinner those with access to diplomatic
shopping will serve good wine brought around by many
immaculately uniformed house servants. The food will
be an approximation of European but made with a mixture of supplies from the same diplomatic stores and
local vegetables and seasonings. Whether it's dinner or a
drinks party, the mix of guests is likely to be diplomatic,
aid, industry and some eminent Bangladeshi political,
business or media people. Usually I'll stop over afterwards with friends. I'm not really on any local social cir-

cuit but it's great to be able to get away and go out sometimes.

Then there's the BAGHA club – the British Aid
Guest House Association – in the same tranquil area. It's a
social club and guest house for British citizens working for
aid projects. I'd go there much more often if it wasn't so
difficult to fit in a visit amidst all the errands I invariably
have to run when I'm in Dhaka. Visits have to be arranged
around work but I always look forward to them. There's a
swimming pool, tennis courts, lovely gardens, a bar and
they make great toasted cheese and tomato sandwiches!

It's also a good place for catching up on gossip and
networking. Put the word out that you're looking for a
supply of medicine or someone to help with a special project and chances are that next time you call by someone
will put you in touch with exactly the person you need to
speak to.

I don't tend to get to know people well as my visits
are rare but it's an oasis of civilization. Unfortunately,
much as I'd like to spend more time by the pool or in the
library, there is so much to do when I'm in Dhaka there's
rarely much time. Sometimes the nurse will take a child to
hospital and I will come and sit by the pool with a cool
beer for a while. I used to feel really uncomfortable about
taking this sort of time as it doesn't seem terribly fair on
everyone else. But life isn't fair, if it was I wouldn't be
here, I'd still be asking people on aircraft if they wanted
ice in their gin and tonics. The staff and children certainly
don't begrudge me these breaks. They'd really like me to
have a much better social life.

I'm not good at walking into a room, striking up
conversations with complete strangers and feeling at ease.
As I said before, I'm a bit short on small talk. The expatriate community in Dhaka is small enough for most people
to know all others of their nationality. As I'm not in town
much, and don't get to know people well, I tend to
stay fairly quietly out of the way. However, I've met some

wonderful people and have been given tremendous support and encouragement

It's a huge pleasure to be invited to a luxurious private house and have a good meal with pleasant company, particularly if it's been a while since I've seen friends and family in England. On these evenings I can rely on being offered a comfortable bed in an air-conditioned room and a bathroom with limitless supplies of steaming water. I'm specially fond of John and Marjorie Walker. John is Managing Director of Glaxo, Bangladesh. Dhaka was their first overseas posting and they have thrown themselves into it with great enthusiasm. Marjorie is a member of the British Women's Association and the United Nations Women's Association. She has helped us co-ordinate the supply of lovely knitted sweaters and fabulous quilts for the children that these groups regularly make. Until you live in Bangladesh you don't realize how cold it can get on winter nights or how chilly the children can feel having endured months of stifling heat. John was wonderful during the cyclone of 1991. Vital drugs were supplied by Glaxo, free of charge, and he was down in Chittagong in the terrible, immediate, wake of the disaster to ensure the Glaxo staff were all right and to lend their help to the badly damaged local villages. It was impossible to co-ordinate our relief effort from Sreepur and he allowed us to stay in their premises in Chittagong. A kind and caring man, he's a great exponent of cricket in Bangladesh and tells me that the national side is as good as the country standard in England and getting better all the time. This is particularly good as they've never been exposed to Test Match challenges. They have, however, won the annual Asian cricket tournament, beating teams from India, Pakistan and Singapore. Perhaps in a few years we'll see a side from Bangladesh facing England at Lords. . . .

Glaxo actually opened its first plant in Bangladesh in 1885 and other big pharmaceutical companies followed because Dhaka was (and to some extent still is) a centre for scientific research, nuclear physics in particular. Since the war with West Pakistan during which 3 million Bangladeshis died, Bangladesh has become impoverished and isolated. Even so, the big international companies have retained their factories because the geographical area is seen to be a perfect beach-head for the export of pharmaceuticals throughout the Far East and into the Pacific rim, including Australia. As things have worked out, there have been tremendous benefits for all concerned, including Bangladeshis. The immediate availability of life-saving drugs and medicines has been extremely important to Bangladesh, particularly during each one of its many recent natural disasters.

But I'd be fond of John and Marjorie and others like them whatever line of business they were in. They are warm, kind people and I am lucky to have known them.

13

The Cost of Living

It takes about £11,000 per month to run our entire project. This sum covers food for the 650 or so children and eighty women, salaries for fifty or so staff, electricity, taxes, the cost of running the cars and trucks, clothing the children and women, dealing with all the administration (every ream of paper or pen or paperclip is accounted for) and, very importantly, the routine maintenance of the buildings. The boys who are learning technical skills in the workshop help a lot with minor repairs and breakdowns, but sometimes we have to call in technical experts which can be expensive. We raise a good deal of money by sponsorship. Some people like receiving pictures of and information on a special child, but their money still goes into the general funds. Some sponsors are more interested, or able to be more generous, than others. Some children might not have a sponsor at all. Every sponsor is deeply appreciated, and they are our main means of keeping things going. We send reports and newsletters and three times a year they receive a letter from a different child on the project. We also send pictures of 'their' child, so the personal contact exists – but money and gifts are pooled, so that no one child in the village is perceived by others to have particular privileges.

With clothes, for instance, we are often short of underwear for toddlers, so a consignment of little knickers in good condition is more welcome than a brand-new party dress for a ten-year-old. Getting supplies over to Bandladesh is really difficult, and some things do go missing in the post. When people send clothes we ask them where possible to send us things in shades of blue. The girls designed their school uniform (which was donated by a Bangladeshi patron) – a loose, blue-patterned tunic and darker blue baggy trousers, which echoes the traditional shalwar chemise – and they can wear other clothes after school hours, but our supplies are always very basic. It's practical, too, to concentrate on one colour, however mismatched the items may be. Repairs and replacement are easier, and the children do seem to like having something approximating a uniform while they are at school. The girls have tailoring classes and make lots of clothes for themselves and the other children.

The children are very proud of their school uniform although, like any children, they have to be watched to see that it's not adapted and changed with bright scarves and junk jewellery. Like almost every other child in the country, they don't wear shoes even with their uniform. The older boys have sneakers to wear in the workshop, as the floor can be covered with wood shavings and a dropped nail or tool could be dangerous. When the children become teenagers they are given a pair of plastic sandals each. Until then they may never wear shoes at all.

To give you an idea of our needs here are a few items from the weekly shopping list – none of which can yet be produced by our farm or in our own workshop in the quantities that we require:
100 kg rice
595 kg potatoes
154 kg pulses
15 kg ginger
91 kg salt
78 kg oil
60 kg fish

4200 pieces of fruit
1400 eggs
96 boxes of Vim
463 pieces of laundry soap
38 coarse brooms
60 boxes of tooth powder

This is a vastly edited down list, and you can see from some of the odd quantities that we calculate our needs almost to the ounce. Although we buy in bulk wherever we can and shop around the many local markets, buying direct from farm or manufacturer wherever possible, there's no rounding out quantities for the sake of convenience. Every taka counts and we are always strict about thefts – however petty they might seem – from the storerooms and kitchens. If an ayah has been caught once, she gets a very stiff warning. The police are called if the theft was a serious one. If stealing continues there's a real threat of expulsion and if they are caught a third time, they are likely to lose their jobs.

The older children are similarly disciplined, and ultimately threatened with being sent for a month to a village where there is a family member. They are given their bus fare home and we'll take them back after they've done their time, but it isn't fair on the other children here, or the ayahs, if people steal.

The same system of warnings and suspension holds for other serious misdemeanours like vandalism and violence. No hitting of children by staff is ever tolerated. I know it has happened, and if the person is caught they are immediately fired. As the systems settle down, rumours and complaints of hitting are much fewer than they were.

Perhaps this sounds harsh, but it's really not possible to run a children's village like ours without a set of rules that everyone understands and which must, if necessary, be enforced. I always hate getting involved in punishments, but there is a need for a framework of rules. It seems ironic to me now that, having got involved with the project in the first place for such positive reasons, I now seem to have to say 'No' dozens of times a day. The children and the mothers are constantly trying to extend the boundaries of what is and isn't allowed, so essential rules must be rigidly maintained: bending of one rule will lead to the breaching of ten others.

For example, we have been given a television and once, whilst I was off the project, the older children pleaded to be allowed to see a movie that was screened outside the hours during which television is allowed. The usual rule was waived. Two days later there was something else they wanted to watch. Two weeks later they were practically glued to the television and refusing to go to school. The volunteer who was in charge of things practically had a riot on her hands, and I was sent a desperate message to come back sooner than I'd planned. It's a real pain to be so strict and to come back in and immediately have to lay down the law.

Sometimes visitors to the village comment that it looks institutional. They're right, of course, because it *is* an institution. By the standards of modern schools in England, with children's wards in good hospitals – let alone most people's idea of domestic comfort – the place is somewhat wanting. But, counting staff, we do have about eight hundred people here, most of them living in dormitories; and although we're improving all the time our first aim has always been to provide shelter and safety, nourishment and education for a large number of children on a very limited budget. It's bound to be institutional.

At least we're thousands of miles and hundreds of years away from what Victorian institutions were like, with their steep red-brick walls, high windows and draughts. But I suppose that even the architects of those places thought they were creating something appropriate (probably modelled on public schools), and in our way we have tried to make the place as comfortable, functional

111

and appropriate as we could within our financial restrictions.

Visitors often ask me why the children are so strictly segregated after they reach a certain age. Family-based groupings are obviously preferable, but we have to observe both practicalities and the customs of the culture that we work in – we have to compromise. We, it must be remembered, are the visitors in this place and our ideas about how children should be brought up must be secondary to those of the community we wish to become a part of. I'm well aware that there is an enormous paradox here: merely by setting up the village, by being concerned about correct nutrition, health, hygiene and education, for example, we are imposing our own standards. However, there must be balance and a sense of priority. With such large numbers of people hygiene has to come close to the top of the list of priorities. I'm well aware of the importance of community, and we're working on a scheme which will allow women and their children to return to their villages, work on commercially viable projects under our supervision and, I hope, take back with them some of our teaching about nutrition, hygiene and so on. In the meantime it would be a recipe for anarchy if the older girls and boys were not separated at night, if the male staff and female staff did not have separate quarters and if the ayah-mothers were only expected to care for their own babies.

To some the care we offer here is a mixed blessing. I know that Mr Haque, our Field Director, worries about giving the children too much. He's been at Sreepur for three years now, having spent twelve years at a Terres Des Hommes, Switzerland project at Kurigram in northern Bangladesh. Whilst we are all agreed on the necessity of caring for the children's physical welfare and the importance of vocational training as they grow older, he is concerned that, however hard we try to place the older ones in jobs or, as our staff sometimes do in accordance with

Bangladeshi custom, orchestrate marriages for the girls, they will find life after our village very hard. The young people have become used to indoor bathrooms and water from a tap. They won't necessarily find such basic fixtures in their new lives, and it may make it all the harder to adjust outside.

However, we've tried to educate – in every sense – these children up to a standard which will make them conscious of the value of basic hygiene, family planning and nutrition, and maybe strive to do something about that wherever they find themselves later on. If ordinary people, particularly women – working on farms, in industry or in shops, living in village communities or in towns – don't expect and work for basic rights and comforts, what hope is there for the country as a whole?

It's quite true that many of the children are sad when the time comes to leave, which is a natural state of affairs in any averagely happy family. With a bit of luck they will find a way to pay for the soap, books and decent food that they've become used to here. Many by now speak some English, which will help them to find better-than-average work. All the bigger girls will have spent at least six weeks in the kitchens, where they will have learned to cook for themselves and have been taught that if food is not properly prepared and decently cooked it will not only taste bad but will also make people ill.

Our village has a good relationship with many of the local employers and manufacturers, so the children have a fair chance of earning their livings through the welding, carpentry and other technical skills that they have been taught here. Often they go back to their family village, but they seldom return to destitution.

The cleverer girls are encouraged to train as paramedics or nurses, to work with computers, and even teach – and all of them become accomplished in the traditional crafts of weaving and embroidery. I know that some of the girls will go back to living in mud huts and might be dissatisfied, finding it hard to adjust, but I don't know what the answer is. We don't encourage crazy expectations, but at the same time we try to promote the idea of opportunity and self-improvement. We hope to relieve a sense of despair, but at the same time recognize the need the children have to keep in touch with their culture and community.

Every child over the age of two is sent back to his or her village, their roots, for a month every year. If they have nowhere to go, they are sent to the home of another child or member of staff. They don't always want to go (particularly as sending errant children home for a while is associated at the project with naughtiness and punishment). But I think it's important for them to realize that their skills and knowledge can be carried back to the place where their home and family are based. I can only hope that each of them will have been enabled to do better for themselves than their parents did. And by training many of the girls as paramedics they will be able not only to support themselves but to bring information and education to a village community and to acquire some real standing and status in that area as well.

Lots of the children return to visit us after they have left. They do seem to regard the place as home, or at any rate a home. Each child is assessed individually and then trained until they have sufficient skills for us to help them find a job. We are often not sure of their age anyway, so we don't have a set age – they must leave when we think they are ready. They come, sometimes, in holidays from their jobs to help us out for a few days, and proudly report on their progress and achievements. This is wonderful for us and for the other children.

Training and motivating youngsters to go out and become independent is hard anywhere in the world. The children are so used to living in a huge family that they have to learn – by themselves – a whole new set of lessons about surviving without one. We want them to make their

114

own way in life and hope very few will need to come back to us because they are in trouble and need help.

However, all in all, I think we have some cause to take pride in what has been achieved through teamwork, guesswork, hard work and the support we've received in the past few years. Perhaps 80 per cent of the Bangladeshi population lives below the poverty line, which means that a family of five or six have to manage on 500 taka a month – £8 to you and me. A small percentage of the population live better than this, in a tin house with no fridge or TV. A tiny number live in some comfort with a brick apartment, a little more space, a motorbike perhaps and a fridge and telly. A tiny, tiny minority have nice houses, gardens, cars and Western gadgets, but I'm not going to be unrealistic. I'd be satisfied if I thought that the majority of our children could live in the second category and a few lift themselves into the third.

I'm guardedly optimistic about the futures of our children. I see that the medical training we are planning for all our girls will help both them and the communities that they might choose to return to. Skilled and decently paid, they may find themselves able to make the sort of marriage that an orphaned girl with no dowry could never have hoped for before. I don't advocate marriage as an easy answer for them, but I have to accept that this is what their culture regards as normal and right. At least these girls can be a bit choosy and make a reasonable match.

At the same time, as I have said, they can contribute towards better health care in their villages. The geography, climate, roads, resources and systems of Bangladesh being what they are, it will be a long time before things will change much and before there are enough clinics in rural areas. A brilliant Bangladeshi group called Gonoshasthaya Kendra are doing an enormous amount of work in this area, and we hope some of their staff will help train our girls.

I'll always be grateful to people who have

supported us in the past and who will, I hope, continue to do so. But ultimately the changes must come from within Bangladesh. In the long term, hopefully, the correct internal government policies will shift things on their axis and gradually the situation will improve. In the meantime I'm hopeful – despite setbacks and disappointments too numerous to itemize – that what we are doing for a few individuals is constructive and can lead to some of our children knowing enough to campaign for the very political solutions which the destitute of Bangladesh so desperately need.

In the meantime there are still thousands of beggars and millions of destitute people here. Each one of them is a disturbing sight. There are beggars in London too these days, and to witness their plight is no less disturbing. I sometimes meet people who start muttering that old maxim about charity beginning at home, but few who express these sentiments seem to do anything at home either.

We all care, whether it is for our family, our neighbours, our surroundings or just ourselves. Different people have different priorities, but I believe that each deserves respect, and caring should not be limited by geographical or any other boundaries. We do what we can in Sreepur; many other people do what they can in all parts of the world.

14

High Days

We have some really happy, celebratory times at Sreepur, often linked into the school or religious festivals. We celebrate the two Muslim festivals of Eid, the Hindu festival of Dirga Puja and Christmas, as well as things like Independence Day and our annual sports day. These celebrations require a little more planning than the average family gathering or small school event, but it's well worth it for the pleasure the children seem to derive from them.

On Christmas Day in 1990 I was the only European staying at the project. I had expected to feel a bit homesick and nostalgic for the trappings of a traditional English Christmas and its build-up, but in the event I wasn't at all. When the aircrews stayed in Dhaka we used to have an entire volunteer group who came out every Christmas and had lots of fun, so I knew it would be a good day. In fact it was rather liberating being there as the solitary expatriate, without having to consider anyone else. The day started with real luxury – I slept until seven. Then there was a power cut and no water supply. By the time I'd had a shower we were well behind the schedule for the day that had been organized by our headmaster, Mr Rahman.

Although Bangladesh is primarily Muslim, Christmas is widely celebrated as a special day just as it is in many Jewish communities – it's called *Boro Din*, which means Big Day – and there are some Christian children in the village. First of all there were dozens of balloons to blow up, fix to the top of the water tower and eventually release. I'd put on make-up in honour of the occasion, and when one balloon blew up in my face it really hurt my eye. Despite the stinging and eyeshadow smeared everywhere, I had to pretend that all was well so as not to divert the attention of staff who were all mastering the art of balloon blowing-up.

Eventually I was able to get away, wash the make-up off and put a piece of ice on my eye, and then we were ready to set the balloons off. The children went berserk and rushed at the colourful cloud of plastic, bursting most of them, but laughing and shouting all the same. Lots had been saved so that we could give one to each child later. The small number of gas-filled balloons that Mr Rahman had brought were a greater success, as these floated beautifully and unreachably above us in the brilliant blue morning sky.

We'd spent weeks organizing a little bag of treasures for each child. Toddlers had sweets, a balloon of their own, crayons and a photocopied drawing to colour in. The older ones had sweets and a balloon too, a felt-tip pen and some tiny toy. The big girls had the same basic package but a little piece of donated costume jewellery and a sachet of shampoo as well. The ayahs got some scented soap or a pen, a comb and a piece of costume jewellery, while the male staff received a torch and some soap.

The different types of package were colour-coded and placed into enormous lucky dips, with the children lining up in their age groups and fishing for their presents. Inevitably there were some tears – someone had a prettier comb or brighter hair-slide – but in the main it was a great success and the squeals of delight were long and loud. The babies were all supposed to receive a piece of clothing, but at that age I don't suppose a new tee shirt is particularly exciting and most of them were old enough to want toys.

We put some larger toys in each room for them to play with together.

I did well. Families For Children had got me some beautiful freshwater pearls and a jewel box. Claire Taunton gave me some luxurious soap and someone else a plate, decorated with a not very flattering picture of myself. After the present-giving we had coffee and a cake which I'd brought from Dhaka, and soon it was time for lunch. The children had the great treat of goat curry. I did find myself thinking of my family around then. I'd spoken to my parents the day before and was half-hoping to hear from them on this day but, typically, the phone lines were down. Again I felt rather relieved that no volunteers were around: I'd have felt terrible for them not being able to speak to their families.

A bunch of British Airways crew members drove in from Dhaka – all on a four-hour transit stop – bringing clothes for the children, some welcome Christmassy things for me and the staff, mince pies and another cake. They had to leave all too soon. Then there was cold turkey for dinner, Christmas pudding and the Queen's speech at about eight in the evening. The children were enraptured by some special videos we'd brought in and were making an appreciative racket, so I think they enjoyed their day. It was a happy one for all of us. My own Christmas ended, as it had begun, on a note of sublime self-indulgence: one of the crew members had brought a new, unthumbed, glossy magazine for me. I took it to bed and blissfully read it from cover to cover before I slipped into a contented sleep. . . .

The children in our village, especially the older boys, are very keen on sports. In fact, coached by one of their teachers and with occasional visits from Malcolm Walker, a BA employee who is a trained coach, their football team is one of the best in the neighbourhood league. Sreepur has also produced a couple of gymnasts of potentially international class. Dancing interests the girls more, and they have lessons in traditional dance and song. Some of our girls are good enough to become professional classical dancers. They all learn Bengali songs as well as literature and history: I think it is crucial to try and develop a sense of identity within their own culture.

Sports day, for boys and girls of all ages, is just a riot – in the happy sense of the word. There is a month or so of preparation, a special committee, a budget and the added attraction of special guests. In 1990 the local Deputy Commissioner was our guest of honour, and he shared centre-stage with a Bangladeshi pop star whom the children had often seen on television. His was a surprise visit and the kids – especially the older girls – were wildly excited.

The village had been dizzy with anticipation since early morning. Flags and bunting had been hung from trees and poles. Several last-minute trips into town to collect supplies had been necessary, there had been loud experiments with the makeshift microphone system, and many children had been pressed into balloon-blowing duty. The older boys bent two banana trees into an ornamental arch. All the children, divided into four 'houses', had been practising their march past for days. I stood in for the Deputy Commissioner at a very elaborate rehearsal and tried to keep a straight face at the sight of such painfully serious drill.

By the time late afternoon came – with the perfect light and temperature for all the races – everyone was in a fever of anticipation. Those of us in the administration block were formally escorted to the sports ground by an honour guard from our scout troop and then welcomed the VIPs. We all sat under a canopy and watched the races, jumping, PT demonstrations and other sports. We'd made a rostrum for winners in each event and set up a first-aid post, although the only nasty moment came during the ayahs' race when an over-enthusiastic ayah took a tumble. She wasn't hurt, but let everyone fuss over her for a while.

The greatest race of the day was the one between the children in Special Care – several children in wheelchairs, others piggyback with their carers, and the disorientated being led and coaxed in the right direction. They were so excited and buoyed up by the excitement that the race went a bit wrong. Nobody clearly crossed the finishing line ahead of everyone else, but they were such good sports that we gave them all a prize.

The Deputy Commissioner then awarded prizes to all the race winners, there were refreshments for everyone, and at dusk the children sang and danced beautifully for us. Those not participating sat and watched quietly in a tired, happy daze. Planning a day like this is exhausting but so well worth it. The children take part so enthusiastically and it helps them to realize that they really are part of a community.

Obviously these special days are relatively expensive to arrange and we budget for them very carefully.

15

Shohel

One evening I was tired but mired in the usual mountain of paperwork. Although I was in the middle of a good book, I still had a lot to do before I could pick it up. Mosquitos were buzzing but I was anxious not to stop even to get the repellent, and every time I smashed one against my shoulder or leg my ill temper increased. I remember I was working on some sort of report which would explain to sponsors how their donations were deployed, breaking down expenses and trying to present it all in a digestible way. I hate dealing with money and accounts and was not having a good time. In the midst of this bleak mood I was interrupted. Our doctor had arrived. This wasn't one of his scheduled visits, so something must be wrong.

I went into the main office and was told that one of our boys, Shohel, had had an accident and then had to have a middle finger amputated. Shohel is a real head-turner. By any standards he is an incredibly handsome boy: tall for a Bangladeshi, well made and with flashing eyes in a face that might have been carved from some precious wood. He's about fourteen now and destined, I'm sure, to be a right little heart-breaker. The people of Bangladesh are often rather fine-looking and fine-featured, so in this respect there wasn't anything special about Shohel. He's of average intelligence and has a very cheerful personality.

He was only twelve and had been with us for about eight years. Apart from his particular charm and good looks he'd never attracted much attention. He'd never been very naughty or ill, and he was no more and no less than a little boy who'd always been pleasant and good-natured.

Shohel was as lively and energetic as any boy of his age. The accident had happened because the little rascal had been leaning out of the back of our truck. His arm somehow got caught between the truck and the tin roof of some building they were passing and his finger became trapped. Another boy screamed the alarm and Mark, who was driving, took the truck to a hospital. Luckily it was quite near, but Shohel had lost a lot of blood before they got there. He was put on a drip and given an anaesthetic so that the doctor could examine his hand thoroughly. The examination room was very basic and the X-ray machine was not working. Luckily our doctor was on duty and told Mark that he needed permission to amputate the finger, as the tissue damage was extensive and he thought there was a real danger of infection and possibly the loss of the whole hand unless it was tidied up. Mark, who didn't feel he had the authority to say yes or no, was very worried about this decision and went off to have a cigarette. In the meantime the doctor decided what was for the best and removed the finger. Poor Shohel was so heavily doped that he didn't know what was happening.

This is where I came in. The doctor, having done the right thing but without authority, thought he'd better keep the finger to prove that it had been too damaged to save. He was quite frank about the fact that it was a shortage of equipment and facilities that had led to his decision to amputate. So I was asked to go and look at the little boy's finger to confirm that I agreed with his decision. The finger was in the freezer section of the fridge we used for vaccines and drugs. I pointed out that I had no medical qualifications or desire to look at the finger, and that the nurses could offer a sounder opinion. But they insisted that I look so I pretended to glance in the freezer door. I asked how they were going to dispose of the finger, but the nurses said that Shohel had an older brother so we should keep it to show him in case he had any doubts about what had been done. It's not quite the same as the situation in the United States, where doctors are deeply concerned about being sued, but they weren't taking any chances.

The next day Shohel had to be told that he had lost his finger – he had such a big bandage and had been in such shock that he hadn't realized. In a way this was the most poignant moment of all. He was brought to the examination room in our clinic, where the doctor quite brusquely told him that he was lucky to have kept his hand. Even with antibiotic injections soft tissue infections can be very serious here. Shohel seemed to understand all this, even though I'm not sure he entirely took it in. He just moved his head to one side in a gesture of acceptance and even smiled at me as he left the room. He laughed and bantered and was soon afterwards persuaded by his friends to ask for the ultimate concession – a pack of playing cards. Somehow seeing him sitting playing cards on a mattress on the floor made me think of the comfortable sheeted bed, TV and video games that the little boy of a friend at home had when he was sick.

Shohel asked for a new pair of trousers as his others were bloodstained. We found that the back pockets of his old pair were crammed with stolen biscuits – just another thing which emphasizes how young he was. That Shohel accepted his wound without a shred of self-pity made it all seem doubly unjust. Anger about the fates doesn't seem to exist very much in Bangladesh. Terrible things happen to many people but are accepted stoically, and the outraged cry of 'Why me?' is seldom heard. I suppose living in Bangladesh does not allow the dubious luxury of indulging in self-pity for long.

In a way the very fact that Shohel's accident was not so serious and could be paralleled with something happening to a child I knew in England made us more aware of our deficiencies than much more serious illnesses could have. His finger could so easily have been saved with the right facilities. This seems a good opportunity to describe the hospital, which is one of Dhaka's best, that he went to for this operation.

As you walk in the entrance the crowding is so great that patients and their relatives are sitting on the steps and lining each side of the corridor. The vast mass of people meant that the cleaner who was trying to mop down the corridor could not do it properly – it was filthy and smelt strongly of excrement overlaid with the nauseatingly sweet smell of stale blood. Some people looked up at us and mumbled about needing help as nurses rushed around trying desperately to cope with at least the most serious cases. The lighting was poor and flies buzzed around.

The wards were just as busy; part of the problem is that there are so few nurses that each patient has to bring their own carer, so the number of people immediately trebles or quadruples. The Bangladeshis are also very family-oriented and sometimes five or six members of the family will come with a sick person to make sure he or she is all right. Often these families cluster round a sick person's bedside, providing food, washing them and even fetching their medication from the nurses. Linen is changed in a loving but haphazard way, and it's better not to think about what happens to the bed pans. It's almost impossible for the medical staff to maintain a hygienic atmosphere in such conditions, but they certainly try their best.

Once, before we moved from Indira Road to Sreepur, we had a real emergency with one of the babies. At the time we relied upon a trusty old Vauxhall, twenty years old if she was a day, for our transport. It was long before British Airways and the Canadian High Commission each gave us splendid Mitsubishi four-wheel-drive vehicles. Anyway, that night the poor old girl let us down and wouldn't start. It was a filthy night, pelting down, and the baby was already on a drip. We just had to get to the hospital.

We stood at the top of our track and had little doubt there would be a bicycle rickshaw at once and that the driver would obligingly let us all pile in and race us to the hospital. The journey was terrible, even though I can smile about it now. We took it in turns to hold the baby, and someone had to hold the drip high enough above the canopy of the rickshaw for it to work. Whichever one of us was holding up the drip had her aching arms drenched, and I'm ashamed to say that by the time we arrived at the hospital we were all hysterical with laughter. I expect this sort of reaction is normal when you are under stress, and I'm pretty sure we couldn't have coped with that nightmare drive without a sense of the ridiculous.

Luckily we got there in time and the baby was soon well again. But we wouldn't have got there at all without the rickshaw driver at the top of the track in the middle of the night.

We take children into Dhaka for hospital treatment whenever there's an emergency that is beyond our clinic's facilities or that of the local doctor. He makes three scheduled visits each week, and we call upon him if we have a crisis at other times. Sometimes there are situations where hospital care is needed. No community of over six hundred children is going to be able to avoid fractures and accidents, as in Shohel's case. Routine children's illnesses like measles can develop complications, and in a country like Bangladesh you have to be alert for the first signs of cholera, malaria, polio, hepatitis and tetanus. But I'm afraid I've got a 'rather you than me' attitude towards anyone who is hospitalized in Dhaka. The administrators, doctors and nurses try their best, but their resources are horribly stretched. There just aren't enough medical personnel, money or nurses to go round.

It's always difficult leaving a child in hospital, but the doctors are exceptional and either the child's mother or a trained ayah goes with him or her. When Shohel went to hospital on the second occasion it was in the company of the most experienced clinic ayah. Shohel had another bone removed, but recovered very quickly. We discharge children from hospital as soon as possible and take them up to our clinic, where the caring facilities are probably better. So he was soon up at Sreepur again and not long afterwards playing football. The doctor is sure there won't be any further complications, and Shohel himself is deciding which vocational training course to specialize in – motor mechanics being the most likely at the moment.

16

The Real Rewards

We're very proud of every child in the village, but many families include youngsters who are extraordinary and we are no exception. Every child and adult in the village is aware of the achievements of two of our boys, Dulal and Mitu, and proud of them. I first met them in the late eighties when I was working at Indira Road. They seemed to be two fairly average boys, perhaps unusually outgoing and well-built for their ages (Mitu is two years older than Dulal), and it was someone else who spotted their potential and carved the way towards a really bright future for both of them.

Indira Road is close to the National Assembly buildings in Dhaka, and in the early morning the children were allowed to exercise and play in the grounds. An instructor in karate and gymnastics, a Mr Juil, saw how athletic Dulal and Mitu were and offered to train them in gymnastics and karate. They were very keen, worked hard and were subsequently asked to participate in a Victory Day competition and display against very tough opposition. Dulal won two first places in gymnastic events and Mitu a second and a third in the karate competitions. The next year Dulal was the national junior gymnastics champion and Mitu won several national karate contests. They were thrilled and so were we, for these awards led to an offer for the boys to continue their education and training at the BKSP – the national sports school of Bangladesh.

The boys are such good friends that, despite their age difference, they are starting at their new school in the same class. They are also very nice boys and we are all so fond of them and proud of their achievements and of the fact that, perhaps more importantly, they have worked and won their way through to the best education that Bangladesh can offer. Even if they are unlucky, or don't fulfil their gymnastic promise, they will have been a marvellous example and some sort of proof that natural ability can be recognized and that such abilities are not always the prerogative of those brought up to privilege. They stay with us during the school holidays – usually we have internal football tournaments going then, and all the teams fight to have Dulal and Mitu in their side. We're trying to get a sports master from their school to come and work for us so that we can improve our physical eduation training. There must be lots of unspotted talent amongst our children.

Dulal and Mitu are a great example of where talent and a lot of hard work can lead. They'd written asking me to come to their first Parents' Day at the school, but I kept in the background as I didn't want to embarrass them, in front of the obviously affluent other students, by highlighting the fact that they came from an orphanage. I needn't have worried. They rushed up and hugged me and were full of excitement as they showed me round the school. They introduced me to everyone we met as their guardian, and I think I puffed up with pride a little more each time! They were obviously held in great esteem by students and teachers alike.

We are already speculating about how each of them will perform at the next Olympics or the next but one. They are an inspiration to all the other children and to our sponsors, but imagine if either or both of them proved to be a world-class athlete!

Another much loved 'Old Boy' is Alal, who left us

in 1990. He's nearly twenty now and doing well in the army. In Bangladesh to be recruited into the army is a great honour, and for every applicant there are many disappointed rejects. Alal is tall and an open-hearted, intelligent young man. Whenever he's on leave he comes back to visit us at Sreepur and help. He's become a bit of a military disciplinarian since he joined the army, and has the nerve to say that we should have been stricter with him! That's a great comment, as I remember what a terror he was when he was younger and the number of times we had such confrontations with him we almost despaired.

Alal was hopeless at school and didn't make any effort to improve. He came from the usual sort of tragically broken home, but his situation was no worse than that of most of the children. Alal's problems weren't any less painful to him for being common ones, and we don't have the facilities to offer special psychological help – which we often thought he needed. He was sent home to his village – our ultimate punishment – for stealing and then almost expelled. He broke into the kitchen store and tried to sell some food outside. Although he made friends easily he was wary of any authority figures, especially foreigners, and rebelled against all rules and systems.

Looking back, I think it was the move to Sreepur that made all the difference. As one of the older boys, by then, he was in the first wave of children who settled in and helped to prepare the place for the younger ones. He immediately took to helping to make the bunks and desks in the workshop, and perhaps the pioneering spirit of that early time in Sreepur brought out the best in him. Alal certainly improved beyond expectations, and was becoming responsible as well as likeable when disaster struck. It was only days before the opening ceremony at the village (by which time we had actually been living there for some weeks). He was in our truck on the dirt road when it went off the edge of the track. Alal was flung on to the ground and a full barrel of diesel fuel fell on top of him. His skull

looked crushed and bloody and he was deeply unconscious.

His great friend, Hatem, saved him by pulling him
out from under the diesel drum, but it rolled over and
Hatem broke his arm in the process. They were both rushed
to the local hospital, which is not well equipped. He had
compound skull fractures and was not expected to live.

An odd coincidence probably saved his life.
Because of the forthcoming opening ceremony Sandra was
in Bangladesh and happened to visit the hospital with a
doctor from Canada. She recognized our boys, and the
doctor was able to arrange for Alal's immediate transfer to
a specialist hospital in Dhaka. The conditions there were
still basic, but it had a staff of skilled doctors. The BBC was
in Sreepur to film the opening ceremony, and their
minibus took Hatem to the orthopaedic hospital where his
arm was dealt with.

Alal fought for his life for days, and one of our
nurses was with him constantly. Iain and Vivienne, my
brother and sister, who were also in Sreepur for the opening ceremony, sat with him one night so that the nurse
could get some sleep. My sister is a qualified nurse and
had helped make him comfortable when he was initially
admitted. After working in hygienic, well-equipped
London teaching hospitals the conditions in the ward
must have seemed even more shocking to her than to the
rest of us, but both of them stuck it out and sat either side
of Alal's bed all night. Tests and X-rays showed that he
had compound skull fractures with a piece of bone pressing on the brain and the doctors thought he would die.

We watched and hoped. Eventually he regained
consciousness and, with the resilience of youth, started to
recover. You can imagine how spoilt he and Hatem were
when they were both well enough to return to Sreepur.
Hatem's arm healed quickly, but Alal's convalescence
lasted several months and he suffered from double vision
for more than a year.

Eighteen months after the accident, still with some vision problems, he applied to enter the army. We were worried that he would fail his physical – that there might be some residual damage. Luckily the army medical showed that he had mended fully, and by now he was so reformed a character that he was accepted almost immediately. He's now a duty assistant in the medical corps and is ambitious enough to have signed on for twenty-one years.

Alal writes wonderful letters to us at the village and says he still regards it as his home. When he comes to stay he helps the children with some of their lessons and runs an army exercise session early each morning. He barks orders like a traditional sergeant major and the older boys love it. They all look up to him and he's a great help in improving discipline – reformed rogues often are. He and Hatem are still the best of friends – the accident strengthened a bond which already existed. Hatem and several other older boys are planning to try and join Alal in the army when they are old enough.

There's a little girl called Rabia staying with us at the moment, although with any luck she'll be staying somewhere else before long. She's utterly charming, and being deaf can ignore all reprimands. She laughs at us when we try and tell her how naughty she has been, and by pretending not to understand she gets away with a lot more than she should be allowed to. She didn't have the best start in life, so her brimming good nature is all the more extraordinary.

Her father was a beggar. He died in 1989. Her mother remarried, but her stepfather maltreated his stepchildren and when she came to us, abandoned soon afterwards by her mother who simply stopped visiting, she was a tiny, malnourished scrap.

Rabia's still small for her age – she's nine but she looks about six – but she's made great strides with her speech and learning. She's certainly able to make herself understood, and she's so clever and intelligent that she has already passed the exam of a special school for bright children with hearing problems. She's lively, good at paperwork and very, very mischievous – the sort of child whose spirit and intelligence are bound to take her forward into a useful and fulfilling life.

With her handicaps, though, she's even less likely than the other girls we care for to make a good marriage. In a society where girls have trouble finding husbands if they don't bring a dowry with them it's terribly important to train them to be self-sufficient. Maybe with time and encouragement we can give the mothers of babies and toddlers enough training to enable them to find decent jobs and to look after their children themselves. We'll also concentrate our resources on equipping older children for the big bad world. Our long-term plan is to have an intensive programme of women's training so that the mothers and their children stay with us for relatively short periods and we can then help to set them up in small cottage industries outside our village. There would be perhaps six mothers and their children in each community. The women will have been taught to read and write, given some vocational skills and numeracy. They will know that, especially during the early stages, they can turn to us if they need help. This will take time and it may not work. We will start with one group and keep on adapting the structure of the programme until we find a way to make it work.

When I'm working in Sreepur all my concentration and energy has to go into the problems, the things that still need to be done. Sitting and writing about children who are doing all right offers a rare and encouraging opportunity to think about successes – a reminder that we have managed to help at least these few youngsters, and a reminder of what special individuals so many of the children here are.

17

The Fame Game

One of the reasons that enough money was raised to build the village at Sreepur is that it appealed to the media. Half the story was already written. Someone with a 'glamour' job, a good salary and first-class everything whenever she travels throws it all in and trades off her luxuries to live in squalor and care for destitute children.

This inaccurate over-simplification, condensing all that has happened, really bothered me. I've always objected to the easy 'Angel of the Airways' label that is so frequently attached to me. I'm only too well aware that I may come across as graceless and churlish at times – I'm just not comfortable with that martyred angel image. What has been achieved at Sreepur is remarkable it's because it has all been achieved by normally selfish and ordinary people who have worked very hard. That, if anything, is a greater triumph than if it had been achieved by martyrs or saints.

I have had any number of arguments with journalists but I am full of gratitude to the writers and photographers who have brought our work in Bangladesh to the attention of the public. The money that has been raised as a result of their work has been, quite literally, life-saving. Many supposedly hard-bitten journalists and photographers have kept in touch, many have sponsored children, others have raised funds and yet others have encouraged their editors to carry on writing about us.

One example of how much journalists helped us was when James Davies and Harry Dempster from the *Express* came to visit us a few months after we'd moved to Sreepur. Harry's idea was to take pictures of children ecstatically scrambling for balloons, so as to raise money by selling pictures of their winning, happy faces. Only it didn't work out. There weren't quite enough balloons to go around, and it turned into a bit of a scuffle with more tears than smiles. It took great patience and a lot of time to see through the chaos and get good pictures.

We desperately needed to repair the mud track which led to the project, and when the two journalists went home they launched an appeal for *Express* readers to help us build a road. They raised £14,000, which enabled us to bridge some gullies and prepare the surface so that when the government team came to build the road they could start right away. Other contributions have been less obvious but no less appreciated – for instance, both of the photographers whose work appears on the jacket of this book are donating their fees to the charity.

On a personal angle, what doesn't appear in the papers is that when I chose to do this work I was grabbing a chance to do something I'd always wanted: learn about another culture and immerse myself in it. The job has given me back, ounce for ounce, more than I have put in, and lots of people who either didn't have the opportunity or just didn't want to could have done it just as well as or better than me. When I've had enough I'll go dancing again, drink as much Chablis as I feel like and eat meat that I've bought, neatly sanitized and wrapped in clingfilm, from some supermarket. I'll go to late-night jazz clubs and dinner parties and revel in having a social life again. Until then, I'm here and doing my level best.

One of the exciting things that has happened has been being awarded an MBE in 1990. This was an enormous honour and a great recognition of the project, but I can honestly say that the person who derived the most pleasure and excitement from it was my grandfather. He was difficult at times, but he did seem to take huge personal pride in my work. He flew from Cornwall to London – the first time he'd been on a plane – when I appeared on the Terry Wogan show. Long before take-off, everyone in the departure lounge knew where he was going and why, as did everyone in the studio queue a little later on.

I wore by BA uniform to accept the award, because I was basically the figurehead for the British Airways staff project. Whilst I had got things going, it didn't seem quite right to take an individual's credit for all that teamwork. As it worked out the uniform was recognized and I was singled out for quite a few photographs and interviews, which all helped the fund-raising. I know my parents felt terrifically proud and I was pleased for them. I also had some fun before and after the ceremony, because I'd looked after members of the royal household on a tour the Queen had made a number of years before.

It had been another great honour – only achieved because I was involved in Bangladesh – to be selected to work on the plane which was used on this tour to Africa, Bangladesh and India. A number of the staff at Buckingham Palace had accompanied the Queen, and as the tour had lasted for several weeks we had all got to know each other. Quite a few people had been to visit Indira Road whilst Her Majesty was on official business. Someone had even got permission from the Queen to give the children a huge cake which had been made for her. The upshot was that, as we walked around with great formality, the odd red-coated footman, standing at attention, unbent and said, 'Is that Pat?' Word went round, and several members of staff came up afterwards and congratulated me on the award. I think they quite enjoyed seeing someone who had been serving them drinks a while before in this different role!

I've since learned of the ongoing value of having

an award such as an MBE. For organizations like ours it has great value, which is, perhaps, at least part of the point of such an accolade.

In Bangladesh, for a start, people often assume that those three letters after my name in a letter or on my card signify some sort of degree. There's a strange snobbery about such things, and it's often helpful to be perceived as a highly educated person.

When Edwina Currie visited Bangladesh I attended a function held for her group at the British High Commission in Dhaka. I didn't meet her, but later I wrote saying I had been at the function and asking her to attend a fund-raising event that Tommy Miah was holding in Edinburgh. In her case she was already interested in Bangladesh and enthusiastic to give her support.

But there must be occasions when being able to sign myself 'MBE' gets my letter a bit higher on someone's pending pile. It's a possibility, and whilst I do feel it's probably unfair I accepted the honour on behalf of the children at Sreepur as well as my British Airways friends. So I have no compunction about using it on their behalf.

After the cyclone in 1991 I wrote to the then Foreign Secretary, Douglas Hurd. I had been so moved by the care, resources and efficiency offered to the people of the stricken Chittagong area by the US Marines and British Navy that I thought the idea of some kind of international co-ordinating of military facilities in disaster areas could be considered. 'The self-sufficiency and discipline for combat seem to be exactly the qualities needed in disaster situations,' I wrote, enumerating the importance of the many facilities that an army or navy in transit has on hand – from a communications network to survey facilities and field rations. Transport is probably the most valuable of all the services that they can provide. 'The point of this letter is to propose that the G7 countries consider a resolution to the effect that any military force present within a certain radius of a natural disaster, and not engaged in essential activities, offer their help to the government of the country in which the disaster occurs.'

It seems to me, particularly as disasters such as cyclones, typhoons, floods and earthquakes generally seem to affect peoples with limited means of helping themselves, that we should all help as much as we can. Efficient military resources could do so much and so quickly if there was an international agreement to get to the affected area with all speed and utilize the training, experience and compassion of the men involved. It would be cost-effective in terms of more conventional relief efforts, since that army or naval force or whatever would have to be sustained anyway.

Mr Hurd passed the letter on to Linda Chalker, Minister for Overseas Development, who wrote back to me with details of the extensive disaster relief plans that had already been made by her ministry.

I also wonder if more major companies could, as British Airways did, get behind aid projects with practical as well as financial assistance. Some years ago I put a suggestion to British Airways that they linked into the major disaster relief charities and set up a regular system to carry emergency goods on scheduled services. They too already had other plans underway.

It's probably a pain when people like me write in, and since I only know a very small part of the picture my suggestions are unlikely to be practicable. Still, it doesn't hurt to try, and there are many times when giving support to charities can also be a form of enlightened self-interest. As far as our project is concerned, it couldn't have been thought of without BA's support; but I would like to think that, in public relations terms, it brought the airline some benefit.

It doesn't come naturally to me to be a focus of attention. I've always been interested in people who are artistic or musical. Although I don't have talent in either sphere myself, I like to spend time in creative environments. I've always been a watcher and listener without making any attempt to go for centre-stage. As a child I dreaded being taken to pantomimes, especially if we had seats near the front, in case I was the 'lucky' one pointed to and chosen to join Widow Twanky on the boards. Can you imagine someone having to give speeches and to talk on the radio and television who used to be consumed with nerves waiting to say 'Here' when her name was called in school assembly?

I've also found the responsibility of the personal attention I've received as a result of my work at the village hard to take. The way the three BBC documentaries focused upon me tended to make it all look like some heroic one-woman effort. Selfishly, the worst thing about it was that if the viewers didn't happen to like me then they wouldn't help the kids, and that responsibility seemed a bit much. At one point, just after the films were broadcast, I took to my bed and hid, not even answering the telephone for several days. Having said all that, the response to the TV programme and the money that came flooding in afterwards were just fantastic.

But I do find it hard being a front person. As a stewardess I was, in a sense, on stage and I came to give quite adequate performances when I was flying. But the difference is that for those finite hours I always knew my lines, was protected by a routine and uniform, and had been trained to cope with almost every kind of question or emergency. As the front person at the village I'm expected to represent the project, and my life's much more boring as I have to be careful not to do or say anything controversial in case people object and then won't help the children. At the height of the publicity I felt under pressure to be nice at all times to everyone. Sometimes I'd get back home, close the door behind me and scream.

It's only right to put my best foot forward when it comes to publicity and fund-raising, and I think that I have done it as well as I could. I owe it to the people who have collected money for us to make the project work, spend their money wisely and be a visible, tangible representative of the village and the children they have worked so hard to help. None the less, I don't find after-dinner or any other sort of speeches easy. I do it. It's as much part of my job as serving dinner was when I was flying, and I've even become quite good at it. But I don't have to claim to enjoy it. We all have our skills and other people are certainly better than I at the fund-raising side, the organizing and badgering that goes into setting up events and carrying them off.

These days, now that the publicity has died down a bit it's much more fun. I often meet people who vaguely recognize my face and think they know me or that we've met before, and I really enjoy the friendly smiles and 'Hallos' that slight recognition puts my way.

Limelight is an odd thing. People (usually actors) say you develop an addiction to it, but this hasn't happened to me – which is just as well as I'm not in it any more. I am relatively unambitious and enjoy time to myself as well as having enough money, a few luxuries and regular sleep. Sometimes it's a strain trying to balance the two lives: being Pat Mummy to the children who see me as a person on whom their welfare depends and the jack-booted boss who has to sort out the politics, against being the stewardess-cum-do-gooder that's seen at home. I'm lucky that I love to read – I almost always carry a handbag big enough to hold a book. Anywhere and any time I can escape to some wonderfully advanced, unreal world where the good guy always wins.

We've been lucky to have such positive media coverage. I have also genuinely encountered no element of competition between the various aid organizations in Bangladesh – in fact we all co-operate and share resources – there are people, however, who simply disagree with us on how different issues should be answered.

We've had criticisms, many of which have been

constructive and well deserved. A number of years ago a leading woman member of the British community told BA that her group could not give us any support because I flew in, stayed in a plush hotel and played orphanages for a few hours each day until I got bored and flew out. Wherever you go, whatever you do, if you do anything at all some people will object. Another rumour was that I only came to Dhaka so much in the first place because I had a boyfriend there. No such luck!

I'm only too aware of my negative potential as an enthusiastic amateur, which is why I've consulted professionals at every turn and have recruited a management team of trained Bangladeshi staff. There really has only been one person in Bangladesh, whom I have obviously offended in some way, who has been consistently negative. She has caused a lot of extra stress by regularly circulating her criticisms, verbally and on paper. I think she means to help and genuinely has no idea of the damage, both in a practical way and in terms of morale, that she has done. On the whole I think it's best to ignore things I can't do anything about, whilst taking constructive criticism on board. There are still difficulties to be overcome, but I'm sure that time will show that the village is well run and achieving its aims.

You have to keep a sense of humour and proportion about the inevitability of things like this. There's a cliché that 'If you stick your head above the horizon you'll be shot at' – but I've been lucky and taken very little flak.

Bangladesh needs to be so industrially vitalized and matters of trade need to be so fundamentally rethought that it will be a while before its government is able to make sufficient internal improvements. There is a valid argument that as a nation it would ultimately benefit by being left to develop without the economic and social distortions that International Aid brings. Practically, aid is not going to be withdrawn – the rest of the world could not sit back and watch the immediate cost in terms of human suffering. Let's hope there comes a time when International Aid and organizations like FFC are no longer necessary.

I realize that much of what I say may sound heartless. Working out here has changed me from an idealist to a pragmatist, but I do again want to make the point that ordinary people like me, grumpy from time to time, with other interests – priorities, even, that they may resent having to set aside temporarily – can take action and be effective. When I read about people who have done things they always sound exceptional – they were either geniuses or flunked out of school. Well, I always had solid 'average' to 'above-average' marks at school and wasn't any trouble or any great asset. It's great to do something; it doesn't have to be a life's work and it doesn't have to be something that gives you a satisfied glow every time your head hits the pillow at night. Of course I'm elated sometimes, and occasionally triumphant and thrilled, but mostly I get on with the daily grind of things that have to be done. I think this is fine (especially since many people loathe and abominate about 98 per cent of their working day). I'm privileged – often annoyed, exasperated, frustrated and depressed, but never bored. I'm totally convinced that many people don't realize their potential and could do much more than they may imagine themselves capable of. All it would take is motivation to take the first step, which has to be a small one, then being prepared to move slowly, work hard and be flexible.

Sometimes we all need a shove. I've never been religious and there are no holy people in my family: it's just a question of opening your eyes. If a derelict called at you in the street the chances are you'd hurry past or at the most fling the loose silver you had in your pocket into his hand. But if someone who lived with you became distressed they couldn't be ignored. You would be involved and try to help them. There's a big difference, I think, between ignoring destitution on the street or at a distance and having to confront it at home. What happened to me was that I spent some time with Families For Children, felt comfortable and then saw, in my home as it were, people who had desperate lives. All I did was recognize this, as pretty much any caring human being would.

18

Monika

Of all the children who have stayed with us, the one whom I remember with the most affection is Monika. She was about six years old when she came to us – but so tiny, weighing little more than 20 lb, that she looked about three. The family circumstances were tragic. Her father had deserted the home and remarried in India. Her bereft mother, Shorala (which Puspu told me means 'simple' in Bengali), was being cared for by Monika and her twelve-year-old sister. The sister worked as a servant in Dhaka and so had little time for Shorala, who seemed to have completely fallen to bits.

Monika had been very sick as a baby, and it was miraculous that she had survived this long. She had a heart defect which accounted for her slow growth and although Shorala had finally abandoned village medicines and taken Monika to see a doctor she wouldn't think of admitting her to hospital. Eventually she came to us in Sreepur.

This was one instance where little screening and research were necessary. Of course we checked on the family circumstances. Basically we admit children and often their mothers too if there is clear danger to life and if the child is at risk through lack of food or medical care. Often minor problems like lice and scabies can be treated within the community, and there is a government scheme to administer inoculations against diseases like TB and measles, but this will take time to become fully effective. Frightened and illiterate mothers do not speed things up.

Shorala, appearing at the gate, was desperate. All she knew was that Monika was getting sicker and sicker and she had no idea how to cope. The little ribcage had become distorted and she was riddled with more minor ailments.

We took them into the clinic, sent for a doctor and eventually took them to Dhaka's hospital for cardio-vascular illnesses. We waited all day in the depressing and grubby corridors until Monika was finally examined. She probably had, they said, a ventricular septal defect – known in Britain as a hole in the heart. They gave us a date for tests, and in the meantime Monika and Shorala stayed with us for several weeks.

Back in hospital Monika coped very well. It was very moving to see how cheerful and even naughty this little girl remained throughout her ordeals and how strong her spirit was. Shorala, on the other hand, disintegrated further, if that were possible. She tried to stop the doctors giving Monika injections and interfered whenever she could. Still, Monika endured all her tests and charmed doctors, nurses and other patients despite her confusion and discomfort.

Monika's heart and lungs were so badly damaged as a result of not having been treated before that some of the doctors thought it was too late to operate. So she was discharged again while they decided how to proceed. Without successful surgery Monika had two years at best before turning blue and dying of heart failure. Eventually it was decided to go ahead with surgery, and the poor little scrap was re-admitted again for further tests before the operation.

Now she went downhill very fast, with terrible pains in her chest, a raging temperature and attacks of hysterics whenever she thought someone was coming to hurt her with yet another needle. The sunny disposition had finally succumbed to a secondary infection which prevented the surgeons from proceeding. As the hospital was geared to heart problems, not violent mystery fevers, we thought it would be best if she were treated elsewhere.

Dr Michaelson of the British High Commission had been helping us to arrange blood for her operation (in Bangladesh it is up to the patient's family or friends to provide any necessary blood for an operation. The hospital won't automatically do so.) He was now able to arrange for Monika to be examined by the President of Bangladesh's personal cardiac specialist. She was tested for everything imaginable, and X-rays showed her lungs to be very clogged because of her failing heart. It was difficult for them to see what else was wrong. She was admitted to a children's hospital and put on powerful antibiotics, but she had lost weight and the bright-eyed scamp had become a listless, whimpering shell.

Shorala dealt with her concern in the most upsetting way for all concerned – moaning loudly that Monika was going to die as she cradled her head and, as before, attempting to prevent medicine being administered. When, as it occasionally did, a spark of Monika's old internal bravery flickered it was even more unbearably poignant.

Against all odds she rallied slightly. The fevers became less frequent and less intense, and eventually the hospital staff said that, as they could do no more, we could take her home to the clinic in Dhaka. Quite soon we felt able to take her to Sreepur, where she was carefully watched by our medical staff. She had good days and bad days, but her cheerfulness was returning and she was spoilt outrageously by everyone.

She was put on a special, supplemented diet and had treats which most of the children would only have once or twice a year. The kids generally understand our policy of strict fairness and equality where food is concerned, but there was never any problem with jealousy over Monika's little extras. She'd won them over too. She even had peanuts, her favourite food, specially collected in Dhaka and brought in by one of our drivers.

Slowly she put on weight, breathed more easily and became stronger. She could totter a few steps, having previously had to be carried everywhere. Then she began to walk properly and became a bewitching little madam as she demanded treats or showed off her new shoes. Sandals in good condition are limited and greatly prized, and these white ones were the first shoes Monika had ever owned.

We were careful to protect her from any virus that might be going around, but didn't want her to live in an incubator. Soon, although she was so tiny, she had established herself as a bossy little ringleader in pranks and games. Even the biggest boys gave in to her charm, tolerated and even indulged her demands. I think it must have been the first time in her life that Monika had basked in affection and attention, and she learned something about playing games and childish excitements. The pinched, prematurely mature cast to her features was vanishing and she began to look almost healthy. Diet, medicine, care and companionship were working wonders, but the principal reason for her blooming, I'm sure, was her own extraordinary inner strength and bravery.

Now that she had pulled through the infection we had to think again about the original problem and the possibility of surgery. We were reluctant to have her re-admitted to the original hospital in Dhaka. The medical care is very good, but day-to-day hygiene and nursing standards are not. With families of patients rather than trained nursing staff often dealing with the sick people, hygiene levels that permit cockroaches and other pests – and limited finances to combat them – ward infections are common and we couldn't put Monika at any more risk. Once again I enlisted the help of Dr Michaelson and he was able to arrange for her to be seen by doctors at the military hospital, the best in the country. The hospital is on a military cantonment and foreigners are not allowed to enter without permission from Military Intelligence. Shorala and I accompanied Monika for her admission but subsequently it was very difficult for me to visit her. There had been some thought that we should try and get her treated abroad, but everyone agreed that here – where diet and language were familiar, where she could be with her mother and see friends – was the best place for her.

Tests and scans took place over a number of months, giving us time to raise money for her operation. Monika had to be treated as a private patient and we needed to raise £2000. Given that we run the entire project on £11,000 a month, finding the money for Monika was going to be a problem. We have raised funds for one-off expensive items in the past – always making it clear that those donations are going towards something specific rather than towards general running costs – but in this instance, where the time factor was so crucial, I was worried. Then, marvellously, an English family who had visited the project did some impressive fund-raising at home and sent us enough money to cover everything.

We explained what was about to happen to Monika and defrayed a last-minute attempt by Shorala to whisk her back to her village where she would almost certainly have picked up another infection. Instead, the idea of a trip back there afterwards was dangled as a carrot to encourage the little girl's spirits. And she was reminded of all the pretty clothes and toys, all the little surprises that were waiting for her when she came back to the project.

We were required to supply much of the equipment which would be needed for her aftercare, and once again Dr Michaelson came to the rescue. He put us in touch with a company who sold the pieces of equipment we needed and helped us get them out to Bangladesh. The weeks while we waited for the team of surgeons from

Pakistan to arrive were probably some of Monika's happiest. When at last they were ready, I was able to get another pass and take Monika back to hospital.

I really enjoyed being able to spend so much time with just one child, especially such a bright and intelligent one. You sometimes feel yourself being spread very thinly when attention and affection has to be divided with scrupulous fairness among more than six hundred children. Having just one little one asleep on my lap or sprawled around me as we looked at picture books was a rarity and a real pleasure.

When the time came to leave her in hospital Monika was cheerful and unconcerned, more preoccupied with unwrapping a sweet than with my departure. Shorala and one of the Sreepur nurses were with her. We'd raced around acquiring the drugs and blood that Monika would need: I blessed the good old NHS while organizing this. Many of the older girls at Sreepur had volunteered to give blood for Monika; three were in the right blood groups, so we were able to take it from them.

'Pray for me,' one of them had cried. Just as I was about to make a caustic remark about that being a bit much since she was only giving blood, she said she meant I should pray that her blood would help Monika. I felt very proud of her and ashamed of myself.

There was nothing more I could do as I wasn't allowed to stay in the hospital. I sent her some peanuts, but they had to be left by the side of her bed – food wasn't allowed any more, as the operation was set for the next day. I was staying with friends nearby and tried to take my mind off things by doing some work, but I couldn't concentrate and when the phone went at about eleven I jumped for it. The surgeon on the line gave me the frustratingly ambiguous news that the operation had been 'successfully completed', but that they were having trouble getting her heart restarted. He said he'd keep me in touch and hung up.

I spoke to Dr Michaelson, who thought it odd that they should have rung then – he didn't think there had been time to complete the surgery. But he told me not to worry. I felt chilled.

An hour later there was another call from the hospital. Monika was still alive on the machines, but her heart was simply not responding to attempts to get it going.

I was convinced that she might respond if Shorala was with her so I begged for a pass, borrowed a car, collected Shorala and drove to the hospital. It was too late. They had just switched off the machines.

I remember staring at the large patch of blood on the gown that one of the surgeons was still wearing. I asked him to speak in Bengali so that Monika's mother would understand. Shorala went into wails of grief and was led from the room. The hospital staff started talking about unused medicines and the paperwork attached to the whole series of events, but I couldn't take anything in.

Eventually I pulled myself together, asked for a sedative for Shorala and started taking the burial arrangements in hand. I signed bits of paper and we left. I thought it would be a good idea if Shorala was with Lokhi, her elder daughter, but when we tracked her down Shorala was too distraught to recognize her.

So sure had we all been that the operation would be a success that no contingency plans had been laid. It was now evening, and I really didn't know where to take Shorala. Lokhi suggested some friends of hers and after driving around the city for about an hour we located them. I thought it was best if the family could be with people they knew well and understood them and so I left, promising to come back in the morning to help with the funeral. I had to call England to stop some people who were about the launch more fund-raising activities for Monika's convalescence.

The doctors told me that when they opened Monika up the damage was much worse than the tests had shown. Had the surgery been performed when she was a baby, she would have had a normal, healthy life. It was a tragedy of ignorance, not indifference. No one could have loved a daughter more than Shorala did, but women like her in peasant communities just haven't got a clue about how to cope and are simply frightened when other people try to help.

I contacted Sreepur and asked that Monika's death should be announced at morning assembly, followed by one minute of silence. There were a few other formalities that I had to attempt that night but I was so exhausted that I went to bed, cried and slept.

In the morning we made arrangements for the funeral and then went to the hospital to collect her body. Monika was Hindu, and if she had been older or at any rate normal size for her age she would have been burnt. But Hindus bury their very little ones, and someone at the cemetery accepted a bribe so that Monika could be buried there.

There were some nightmare preparations. So frequent are infant deaths in the area that space at the cemetery is at a premium, and we had to watch as the earth cleared for Monika threw up dozens of tiny bones. The ritual of washing her body, three times with perfumed water, was carried out and she was wrapped in a white sheet. Everyone was sobbing by the time Monika was finally laid to rest, the incense lit and the rose water sprinkled on the soil that now covered her. Mr Das and I drove back to Indira Road.

For months after that, during any idle moment at Sreepur and especially at night, I thought about Monika and wondered if we'd made the right decisions. She might have had a year or two longer without our pressing for the surgery. She was missed terribly and will never be forgotten. Once, when I was feeling particularly gloomy about it all, a good-hearted but rather simple-minded ayah pointed out the obvious. 'But look at all these other children. . . .'

Money collected for Monika by schoolchildren in England is being used to set up a small clinic in our Dhaka office. In the longer term, Monika's unnecessary death makes me more convinced than ever that our aim, to train nursing auxiliaries who will return to their villages and gradually help the people there to see that modern medicine is usually more effective than folk remedies and that it is nothing to be frightened of, is a valuable one.

19

The Riot

The unnecessarily sad fate of youngsters like Monika were very distressing and tested our resilience. In our community with eight hundred individuals there were occasionally problems involving larger numbers which threatened the entire project.

The older children had a riot in 1990 and it hurt me deeply.

I'm the last person to expect that day to day life in a community like ours will run with unshakeable, placid goodwill and clockwork precision. Little infights, resentments, crises and dramas are inevitable. Nothing, however, had prepared me for the violence and venom of this mutiny. I felt as if years of pent-up hatred and anger towards the staff were being expressed with a savagery that the children had never expressed before. I had no idea, until then, that such angers even existed. I couldn't help taking it seriously and it was weeks before I felt quite steady walking amongst the children.

We have a system here of issuing warnings to children (and staff) if they are seriously destructive, disruptive or dishonest. If the bad behaviour persists, after three warnings the offender is sent back to a relative or friend in a village for a month. They know that when they come back they are on their last chance and their behaviour usually improves.

Trouble started when two sixteen-year-old boys, Shiraz and Babul, had had their final warnings and their month in their villages. Then they behaved in a way that made staff worried about the younger children. It wasn't that they were physically violent, but they came back full of threats and with the 'big man' swagger of boys who had done their time. Their resentment at their punishment was still very strong and they incited a bunch of older boys. There were thirteen ring leaders and peer-groups pressure being what it is, they had soon enlisted the help and support of most of the older children. The atmosphere became hysterical and quite nasty. The older girls were dragged in and the staff and administration buildings were barricaded. There was chanting and stone-throwing and it was disappointing that most of the Bangladeshi staff were so frightened of the children that they did not help at all. The two errant boys had been told that although we thought they should leave the project we would help them to find work, but even so they still seemed determined to make things as hard as possible for the rest of us.

The children wanted to decide who should stay and who, if anyone, would have to leave. Their shouting and chants indicated many and various dissatisfactions but later, when the atmosphere had cooled a little bit, the grievances seemed pretty trivial: they didn't like the soap we bought for instance. More reasonably, perhaps, they wanted more vocational training. When things were at their fiercest, however, I reluctantly decided to fetch the local police. I still find it hard to believe that some of these children, many of them young boys I had known for almost ten years, could be so violent. I was stunned as I watched one youngster pick up a stone and throw it at the windscreen of the jeep I was driving to the police station and heard another threaten to puncture the tyres. The stone missed by miles and I don't think they can really have wanted to damage me or the car but it was an awful moment. On top of everything else two major donors from the UK, Ted and Nicky Smart, had flown all the way from England, for a few days, to see where their money was going only to be caught up in all of this.

A total of six policemen came and they went with all the older children into a schoolroom, calmed everyone down and listened to complaints. In a different room staff members and I checked the files of the boys who had actively threatened to harm people and ascertained that they all had somewhere to go if we expelled them. We decided that we could not and must not back down on our disciplinary systems if we were to have any hope of keeping the project running properly. We eventually decided to expel the original two plus eleven other ring-leaders, otherwise the children would learn that all they had to do to get what they wanted was to riot and we would have a situation where it could be impossible to keep things going. The police helped us to work out travel arrangements for the culprits and we gave them money for their fares back to relatives in their respective villages and promised to help them find work. Luckily, considering the hundreds of tiny children on the premises, no one had been hurt but we could not tolerate that militant tendency amongst the children. Nothing like it happened before or since.

The next day I discovered that Shiraz and Babul, who were sixteen at the time, had somehow got a fax message through to Sandra in Canada complaining about my disciplinary measures and claiming to be only eleven years old. Sandra had their version of the story first and was initially all for allowing them to stay. Imagine, from her point of view how terrible it must have sounded that I had just thrown them out. Of course, when she heard what had actually happened, she agreed that I had no choice. I had known most of the boys a long time though so it was very hard to see them go in an atmosphere of anger and recrimination.

155

Order was restored and we tried to carry on in a normal way but the whole episode depressed me dreadfully and I felt totally responsible. With the ayahs and the Bangladeshi staff being so passive (Mr Haque was very new then and had tried to help but had been threatened with a knifing), all the decisions beforehand and during had to be mine. No one likes to be unpopular and for some time afterwards my self-confidence was shattered. This, coupled with a great sense of resentment and disappointment towards the children who had shown such anger towards me, made it hard for me to relax with any of them for quite some time. Immediately afterwards most of the children were unhappy and apologetic and made it clear that they were sorry for their behaviour. Most of the boys who had left wrote saying they were sorry they had behaved so stupidly. Several even wrote to siblings telling them to behave and not make the same mistake. All families have rows. Eventually I came to think of the riot as a family explosion, amongst volatile people, on a particularly large scale.

Later I tried to analyze why it had happened. The punishment of two not particularly popular boys amongst six-hundred-odd normally happy children wasn't really enough to explain it

I think the problem was I had tried too hard to give the children self-esteem. This too rapid attempt to instil in them a sense of hope and pride had backfired. The nature of our organization had led to things like our scout troop having its badges awarded by immaculately uniformed members of the Presidential Guard, the football team being so well coached that they were local champions, frequent visits by VIPs and so forth, and had momentarily given the children a great sense of their own importance with no balancing feeling of responsibility. Perhaps, more deeply, it was an expression of fury about the awful circumstances that led them to us in the first place and this was the only way that some buried resentments could be articulated. The instigators were teenagers and most teenagers rebel in some way. Mostly they have naturally sunny dispositions, but all of us have our bad days and there does seem to be a bit of a tendency towards hysteria which can soon get out of hand. I still struggle to find a reason; numerous inquests have led us to make several policy changes and we have done all we can to make sure a similar thing doesn't happen again.

We all respond to peer pressure and charismatic leaders. Bullies rule playgrounds all over the world. The whole horrifying and upsetting business tended to reinforce my view that there should be fair discipline, but in the long term preferably meted out by someone other than me. It'll be wonderful when I can come back, see everyone, help where I can but not be in the driving seat. Pat Aunty, perhaps, rather than Pat Mummy.

20

Rina and Shopna

When I first arrived in Dhaka, among the children who tumbled into the old car that met me at the airport were Rina and Shopna, whom I came to think of as the terrible twins. I remember them with particular clarity because they were so smart and pretty and they made it clear from day one in Dhaka that I was under their wing. About nine years old at the time, they were much naughtier than most of the other children but usually quickly forgiven. They adopted me as their favourite foreigner.

They were born in 1979 and had come to Families For Children six years later, undernourished and ill, when their mother had despaired of being able to give them a decent life. Rina had a little scar on her nose, and it was only by looking for this that you could distinguish between them. They were both fine-featured, with merry dispositions and, as is so often the surprising case, well adjusted. As twins, though, they needed each other terribly and fought, wept, spoke, covered and thought for each other all the time. They were so cute that it hadn't been difficult to find sponsors for them in Canada, and reading the volunteers' reports on them I see, with amusement, how some of their naughtiest behaviour was covered by euphemistic phrases – people only remembered their charms and winning characteristics. Like all the others they had battled their way through chickenpox, mumps, conjunctivitis and all the other childhood ailments, keeping their good humour and playfulness and retaining a sense of specialness, as twins often do.

They hardly ever saw their mother, who lived in a village far from Dhaka. As time passed they became slightly competitive and wanted, rightly, to be treated as individuals. This created a few problems, but again and again if one of them fell ill the other would react in some way, and they were usually neck and neck in their marks at school and place in their class. The closeness and the competition co-existed. As the years passed they became two of the most popular children on the project. I was, as always in cases like this, a little uneasy about my personal fondness. I think it's essential to be scupulously fair to all the children – you can't suppress particular affections, but you must be very careful not to behave with any favouritism. In the 'normal' world everyone takes a greater interest in some people than in others. That's how we choose and keep our friends: we can't care equally about everyone we meet. But I still felt a bit guilty about liking the twins so much.

In their early teens Shopna started to shoot ahead of Rina in school. Rina reacted by working less and opted, as she wasn't going to be the bright twin, to be the noisy one. They argued with each other more and went into a sluggish decline that no one could lift them out of. I suppose this might have been nothing more nor less than the pressures of adolescence and growing apart. In any case, the two of them became unreachable. They became taller and physically more mature, and seemed to lose interest in their studies and their futures. At the end of the school year Shopna was moved up a grade and Rina wasn't. The next year, acquiring separate identities and studying different subjects, they both perked up again. Maybe it was a coincidence or maybe they had a need to establish themselves as separate individuals, but they certainly became close out of school and cheerful and pleasant again.

Thinking about them now, they are a good example of everything working out in the end. Almost all children, including the most placid of babies, will have a time during their childhood or teenage years when they will be difficult. You just have to try and support and sustain them through it. It's great being hugged by a two-year-old but it's even more special if older children of perhaps sixteen can react in the same way.

The girls came through this passage of terrible gloom and things have worked out well for both of them. Shopna trained as a nurse and worked at the Metropolitan Hospital in Dhaka, where she lived in a hostel with other nurses. She has now come back to work in our clinic. Rina trained as a computer operator and lives in Dhaka, with a friend's family. She visits the village and the babies' home in Dhaka quite regularly and both girls see each other, too, without needing those intense bonds of twinship anymore.

Looking back over their files, I see copies of formal little notes which they wrote to their respective sponsors over the years they were with us. I hope the sponsors realized that writing in English is often a great effort for these young ones, and that the brevity and occasional solemnity of the notes is seldom an indication of the child's personality or attitude towards their sponsor. It's simply that they find it difficult to express themselves in a second language with a different alphabet and sentence structure.

Perhaps the main reason to write about Rina and Shopna is that – apart from the fact that they have attractive natures – they are good examples of how children at FFC can follow quite normal paths: promise followed by apparent decline, which is followed in turn by a fulfilment of potential in their own time, at their own pace. It happens all the time in smaller families.

The girls are solid examples of what we aim to achieve on the project – qualified, well adjusted and independent young adults with a decent earning potential.

160

They were both beautiful little dancers as children, particularly graceful in the traditional snake dance which is performed on special occasions at Sreepur. I'm always reminded of those terrible twins when this dramatic traditional dance parable is performed at the village, its dignified movements combining with wonderfully expressive facial gestures. And I'm actually reminded not so much of what we have helped to achieve for them but of how they helped my arrival here to be such a reassuring one. They still see our relationship as special and hand out teasing abuse along with hugs and affection when I'm with them. I'm lucky to know them. Shohel had his drama. Poor little Monika had hers too, but most of the kids grow up with the usual childhood ups and downs, periods of enjoying school, periods of resenting it, times of clinging, times of resenting authority, making friends and breaking friends just like youngsters all over the world. Rina and Shopna are two great children who've overcome their considerable initial disadvantages and become nice young women with decent jobs and some prospects.

As always, we did our best to see that they had somewhere safe to live before they left us and made sure their rent would be paid for a while. And as always, we'll continue to watch their progress. And they – in fact all of our 'exs' – are welcomed back whenever they come to visit.

21

The Cyclone

A great wind blew up on the night of 29 April 1991, and with a windspeed of 150 mph a great tidal surge, in some places twenty feet high, struck a length of coastline in south-east Bangladesh. It hit a stretch 175 miles long, and about 15 million people were affected directly. Its miraculous that 'only' 150,000 people were killed. Half a million survivors lost their possessions, lands and livestock. In some ways the enormity of these figures mediates against enduring sympathy with Bangladesh's plight: the figures are too massive to comprehend.

We knew there had been a warning of the cyclone but that many people would have ignored it because of a fatalism bordering on indifference – also because most people would want to stay so that they could try and save a precious goat or chicken or tin pot or corrugated iron house. There were some cyclone shelters but not nearly enough.

The sheer ferocity of the wind was almost beyond belief as the cyclone crashed into the landmass, and by the morning of 30 April four inches of torrential rain had compounded the wind damage. Massive trees had been uprooted as well as houses destroyed, villages flattened, crops ripped out of the earth. Thatched and tin roofs whipped around in the air. Only a few feet above sea level at the best of times, some of the smaller offshore islands completely disappeared.

In Sreepur we heard rumours of the horror but Chittagong was cut off – no phones, no roads, no communication at all. The BBC World Service started to broadcast some accounts of the tragedy, and we all crouched over the radio for every scrap of news. Bangladeshi radio and newspapers also carried stories, but they differed wildly in every telling. We'd started to organize supplies to send to the government collection spots. All international lines were down, so I couldn't contact the UK or Canada for directions or for extra money, but I knew they'd want us to do all we could. I finally got a call through on a landline to the Families For Children project in India to pass on the message that we were all right.

People can survive if they have certain commodities. They need pure water and containers to hold it (many of the wells and ponds had been contaminated by salt water or by the rotting bodies of the dead). They need food that can be eaten without cooking (fires could not be made out of the few soaking pieces of wood that remained). They need medication (to treat immediate injuries, to try and prevent disease, to deal with the disease you have failed to prevent). And they need clothing and shelter (this is the cyclone season; there are storms with driving wind and rain almost every day).

We lent our truck to the government office to help them move in these desperately needed supplies, and sent down sacks of the raw brown molasses and processed rice called chirra that they were asking for. More accurate reports were coming through now and the government had sent the army in to help: they had the dreadful job of burying the bodies, a task made even worse because the ground was waterlogged. They started burning them but ran out of kerosene. The survivors were numb, searching everywhere for relatives and for any scraps that were left of their homes. People had tried tying themselves to trees – sometimes that worked, and sometimes the entire tree was washed away.

Our nurses are trained in treating large numbers of people: almost all our children are malnourished when we take them in, and the illnesses they catch are the sort of thing you see after a disaster. I offered our help to the government, but was anxious not to rush in without planning as we wanted to help solve problems rather than add to them. Workers and goods were getting into Chittagong and medical and refugee camps had been set up there, but getting out to the stricken islands and coastal areas was still very difficult.

In Dhaka, making final arrangements for our convoy to go down, I phoned my friend John Walker, MD of Glaxo, to make sure he was all right. He'd just come back from the Glaxo factory there which had been spared by a seven-foot-high railway embankment between the buildings and the sea, and the fact that the land there is densely wooded and gave some resistance to the winds. When he heard we were going down he immediately offered us the shelter and water supply of his factory compound. He also arranged for the factory to produce vast quantities of oral saline, a simple mixture of salts that is mixed with pure water and given to people with diarrhoea – and which is literally a life-saver as it prevents dehydration.

We wanted to help with the basics – water-purifying tablets, simple health care and food. We had to take everything we might need with us, from latrine bases and hurricane lamps to blankets, water barrels and food. The truck and a car set off on the eight-hour journey, knowing, thank goodness, that we had a base to organize things from once we got there. We stayed at the Glaxo factory for a day whilst I visited all the large foreign aid and local organizations working in the outlying areas to get together as much information as possible. I spent hours at the government offices with lists of materials and personnel, so that they could decide where we would be most useful.

The minister co-ordinating the relief effort had heard that there was a tiny coastal area called Chanua which had been completely cut off and had not had any medical help at all. Next morning we were airlifted there by several helicopters of the American Task Force operation called Sea Angel. Despite a meeting during which jobs were carefully allocated, several staff decided they knew better ways of making the final arrangements for topping up of food, water and so on. There were plenty of dramas and panics and I thought we were going to start off really well by missing the helicopter, but we got there on time and started loading up.

I went with the second shipment, which was mostly water, and because of another mix-up – this time not our fault – got dropped off in the wrong place. I realized just before the helicopter left again and managed to get the incredibly heavy water loaded back on. The marines were wonderful. They'd just had instructions to drop goods at this site, but took me to a second to check it out. Third time lucky – just as well because the helicopter was getting short of fuel. So we unloaded and started getting set up.

That afternoon we built a latrine and bathroom, sorted out our supplies, put up the tent we would use as a clinic and met the local officials and some other aid workers. We worked out what we could do in the way of pooling resources and in complementing each other's work so that we could all be as effective as possible. Our team then had an evening meal and we organized enough room amongst the stores for everyone to lie down and get some rest.

We slept all together in that one stifling room – all that was left of the school – on mattresses on the floor with mosquitos, hundreds of flies and a sociable rat as well as one sleep talker and one heavy snorer.

At five o'clock the next morning we opened the clinic and started distributing medicines and foodstuffs, giving basic medical care and advice on clean water. Hundreds of people lined up, and the nurses and first aiders worked in shifts with the rest of us backing them up with supplies and keeping records.

In some ways, after a disaster like this, the horror not only continues but gets worse. Water is polluted, sanitation fails, people get diarrhoea, dysentery, chest and skin infections. On that first day we saw almost two hundred people. During our weeks there we treated a total of 7366 people. In the midst of all this the Bangladeshi people did not lose their hospitality – we were invited to one of the few buildings left standing for tea. Carefully laid out next to each of the mixture of cracked cups and glasses from which we were to drink was a biscuit from the concentrated emergency rations. It was all they had to offer, so offer it they did.

I can't truthfully say that our little band had come without some reluctance. It's much easier to be decent to other people if you've had a comfortable life yourself. In Bangladesh there is such social insecurity that anyone – let alone the waifs and destitutes of Sreepur – is understandably more concerned with themselves and their immediate family than with afflicted people hundreds of miles away.

I'd had to bully people a bit to get them down there. I tried to explain the importance of our little effort. The first team weren't so bad, but the conditions were still very poor and the subsequent relief groups weren't too enthusiastic. After the first few days we knew which medicines were the most crucial, and we were already running short of some drugs. I managed to hitch a lift on a helicopter back to Chittagong and went back to Dhaka to sort out how we were going to organize the operation on an ongoing basis. Until we'd actually been in and assessed the area and its needs we hadn't been able to make a long-term plan. We sorted that out, and lots of important details like getting slips which showed the sun's position in the sky which could be marked so that illiterate people knew when to take their drugs. I then went back with further supplies and the next team of workers.

The sea was so rough that boats weren't going, but all the bridges from Chittagong up to about six miles from our camp had been repaired, so we went as far as we could by car and walked the rest. My strongest memory of working down there has to be the nightmare of getting in and out. This time we had to cross a makeshift bamboo bridge to get from one fragile landmass to another, supplies slung across our backs and chests. The bridge was perhaps nine inches wide and crossed about forty feet of heaving water. There was a fragile lacework of ropes to give hand support, but for some reason it was very widely strung. You had to walk across those nine inches with both arms outstretched and gripping the ropes, your load balanced on your back. Beneath you the water frothed and swirled and the bridge itself swayed. I had to march on first, of course, or nobody would have tried it. Walking straight forward I tried not to think, hoping the others were following.

We waded on through mud to reach our semi-stranded community. When we got there, by some wonderful fluke of luck an American boat was there, carrying supplies for the Red Cross, and a kind marine hosed me down. I hope I will never be as filthy again in my life. The marines who had come straight from the Gulf War, were indescribably helpful. They must all have been war-weary, sea-weary and homesick, longing for the swiftest passage back to the States. But throughout their time in Bangladesh they behaved with faultless courtesy and, much more than this, enormous compassion. Above all, there was a recognition of how much their relatively sophisticated resources could help in such a disaster situation. The British Navy were working in another area, although they did divert to bring a pump and fuel in for us, but I am sure they were just as busy and helping just as much.

A couple of weeks later I had to go back to the children's home at Sreepur; by now the third team was in place and the fourth would be coming in a couple of days. Everything was running as well as it possibly could. Whilst almost everyone made a fuss about coming down they were wonderful once they actually got there. They worked long hours with no complaints and were always ready to help if there was an emergency during their few hours off.

I was both sad and glad to be going back as I started on another horrendous journey which soon preoccupied all my thoughts. As a stewardess I've sat on motorways, knowing that my flight was due to leave, and seeing the pounds clock up on the taxi meter as we were stuck in a jam. I've even been on flights where the death of a passenger or a diversion or a technical problem has made being a crew member less than pleasant. As a private individual I've experienced many journeys that I would once have described as horrible.

By now the ferry service had started up again. Going by that rusty steamer from Chanua to Chittagong usually takes six hours. On this night six of us were crunched into a tiny cabin adjacent to a much-used lavatory with no flush. The sea was choppy and we were hours behind schedule. Conversation had been exhausted hours before, and the kind of fatigue that places one well beyond sleep had made zombies of us all.

Approaching Chittagong at last, we were informed that the weather and the vast number of damaged boats across the mooring would prevent our disembarkation. Oddly, after days of chaos this sort of announcement was greeted rather calmly. We were to sail further upriver and meet another boat which would take us on to a smaller jetty. All sounds pretty civilized, yes? In fact we sailed onwards through massively turbulent water, in heavy rain which obscured our vision and made everything slippery. Then we had to climb on to benches, on to the rail and finally leap down into a tiny steamer.

After that we pitched towards a jetty, which turned

out to be an old barge moored near the shore. The water below was rocking violently and the walkway had been washed away. It had been temporarily repaired by balancing single planks between the struts, with no handhold on either side. The planks tipped with every footstep and the sea was only ten feet below us. It was only a forty-foot walk, but it seemed to take forty minutes.

Finally there was dry, or at least damp, land. I felt filthy, smelly but above all relieved to be back in relative civilization. I had a splitting headache which cleared up after gulping a pint of water. I'd become dehydrated because I hadn't drunk enough – probably an unconscious attempt not to have to use that horrible toilet. Most of all I wanted to get home to Sreepur to have a hot shower and make sure that everything there was all right. Our project is built in an area where there are tornados rather than cyclones, but is constructed in such a solid way that it is tornado-proof. Other than the extra work of organizing the relief team, everything there had gone on as normal.

There was so much misery and tragedy so near that it seemed strange to return to a place which was working as it always did. As usual there had been some light moments during the past weeks, such as the tiny children stealing washing from the line because they wanted to give something to the cyclone victims. There were also plans to be made for the future. Profiteers had pushed up the price of the processed rice called *chirra* that could be eaten raw and which was a staple for survivors just after the cyclone. We had been furious and had found that we could install a mill to make it very cheaply. The British High Commission thought it was a good idea and had agreed to finance it. Now we had to organize the paperwork and installation. Next time – unfortunately, there is likely to be a next time – we will be able to make this food at cost price for ourselves and as many other groups as possible.

I'd always longed for adventures as a child, as all

children do. As an adult this wish adapted into an impulse to travel and a growing curiosity about other cultures. For a long time flying with British Airways satisfied these desires. At some level I knew perfectly well that thinking about adventures is usually a mixture of memory, day-dreams, time on one's hands and great surges of energy. I'd now learned that real adventures were always uncomfortable, often boring and occasionally frightening. Selfishly and personally, I hope I don't ever again have to encounter the degree of misery I saw in Chanua. The scale was too great and the attempted solutions too few.

Several days later I was being driven through Dhaka and a minor incident took place in front of me. I saw a boy being beaten. We were in traffic and couldn't stop. I just sat and thought: I don't want to see even this sort of thing so closely any more. Fate determined that I was in a situation, only hours from a cyclone area, with qualified and experienced people who could help. We did what we could and they were simple practicalities. Everything I'd learned in life, including aspects of my British Airways training and experience, were definitely useful. Aircraft discipline: be calm, offer reassurance, be practical, tactful and above all, don't panic. Ironically, tolerance and patience applied to a difficult customer in business class taught one or two lessons which were usefully applied, years later, in Bangladesh.

22

What Next?

I keep my hair very long, which may seem impractical in a climate like that of Bangladesh, but really it isn't. It's easily kept off my face and neck by twisting it into a knot, and if I need to attend some smart function or embassy party I can quickly dress it up myself. There is seldom time or opportunity to go to a hairdresser.

In London I go to a very good hairdresser in the West End once every six months, and also treat myself to a make-up session every couple of years, buying two of each cosmetic recommended. This is an extravagance, but it's also a great time-saver as I then wear pretty much exactly what he suggests. It also considerably reduces the stress involved in suddenly having to look smart if the occasion arises. Knowing that all the kit is to hand and having been shown how to use it gives me a bit more self-confidence if I'm called upon to give a talk or meet important people. I know the way you look shouldn't make any difference – but I also know it does. Anyway, Sreepur isn't exactly the sort of place where you can dash out and buy a lipstick or a pot of face cream if you've run out so having one trusty and complete range to hand helps a lot.

Everyone has little luxuries that they indulge in from time to time. Some are obvious. I remember during the last cyclone getting a call from Mike Osborn, the British Airways manager, to say Lord King's office had

contacted him to ask how we were and if we needed anything. I thought he was joking and facetiously said that a
crate of champagne or Chablis would go down well. Silence
on the other end of the phone soon let me know I'd made a
mistake and I back-tracked hastily with the information
that we were all well and organizing a relief operation. Still,
those beverages were definitely the first luxury to spring to
mind! Realistically, in Sreepur, my indulgences make me
feel better and probably, therefore, able to work more
efficiently. I bring odd things out with me when I come
back from the UK – some Cheddar cheese or an expensive
duty-free perfume or sweet-smelling soap. I almost always
wear nail varnish, however damp and dowdy I might feel;
however harassed and flung together, I allow myself that
concession to vanity and grooming. For my own self-
respect it's important to me to look as good as circumstances allow. Doing this work, in this place, is no reason to
look a mess all the time. In fact in the heat and stress of the
project it can make you feel much better to spend a few
minutes every now and then pampering yourself. Other
people have other ways of coping but being a fairly self-
indulgent creature I enjoy having some time to look after
myself. Sometimes it means getting up very early in the
morning to, say, do my nails and wash my hair. Sometimes
I don't bother for weeks on end but I know some time spent
fussing with my appearance helps me wind down and feel
better so I always have a few pots and bottles of nail varnish, creams and hair conditioners around.

I know that things like keeping my hair long and
having a demonstrable interest in my appearance helps
my relationship with the people I work with. Long hair is
seen as a great asset in Bangladeshi women and the children make it clear that they think it's my one redeeming
feature and that I had better not cut it. Even the little girls
spend hours dressing each other's hair and we encourage
it. Frequent combing and grooming reduce head lice.
Twelve litres of coconut oil is included in our tightly bud-

geted weekly shopping list, so that the girls can massage it into their hair as they would if they were back living in the city or their home village. Having the cherished glossy, thick hair and the odd cheap trinket is very important to most of them, and it would be sheerest folly to discourage such small vanities.

Make-up, again, is traditional in this culture, and from quite a young age the girls will rim their eyes with kohl. So when I do dress up and put on make-up they get excited and proud: as they are fond of me, they want me to look good. In fact they are always delighted and curious when I am going out. Curly hair, too, fascinates them. Sometimes we've had volunteers with wavy hair and the little girls want to touch it and poke their tiny henna-ed fingers through the springy curls – for them as exotic as a Mohican haircut or a green fright wig. They're very critical of women with short hair and sometimes to my great embarrassment make their feelings clearly known.

Far from discouraging self-decoration and small personal vanities, we actively approve of them. We're trying to restore and build self-esteem as well as offer safety and nourishment, and pride in appearance is a significant barometer in the general health of most people. It struck me when I first started working in Dhaka, and it strikes many visitors, how people in the worst quarters of the city or in the poorest villages always look clean and, however miserably deprived, conscious of their clothes and appearance. If we can help to restore and sustain that pride by recognizing the validity of 'trivialities' like henna and kohl, that's fine by me.

On the whole things are running smoothly now, under the control of our Bangladeshi management team. I had never intended to become so deeply involved in the lives of these children and their mothers. Far less did I expect that at least half my time would be taken up with administration and organization, recruiting and overseeing staff.

I want to return to England, although I'm not yet sure what to do next. There are so many things I want to do and see, and, even more importantly, friends I want to spend time with. Resuming my education is a possibility, as is working again as an occupational therapist. Come what may, I want to retain an involvement with the village at Sreepur and be able to visit fairly often. It would also be dishonest to suggest that from time to time I haven't rather resentfully regarded the demands of six hundred-odd Bangladeshi children as an unsatisfactory substitute for one or two of my own. At other times I've felt blessed and lucky to have been part of the lives of so many special people.

Newspaper and television journalists have concentrated on what I regard as only a part of my life. I'll always be grateful, in particular, to the TV programmes which drew attention to the project and for the funds which were raised as a result, but they did have the effect of typecasting me as something that I feel I'm not. I became tangled up in something that engulfed every other aspect of my life, and I want to return to some semblance of normality whilst I'm still young enough to enjoy it.

I'm also fed up with catching minor ailments, tired of being the person who has to say 'No' or 'Stop' or 'Out' or 'Impossible', who is associated with all the unpopular decisions and the problems.

It's a mistake to imagine for a second that an apparently unsophisticated community like that at Sreepur is much less political than Machiavelli's Florence. As in any office, everyone is status conscious – all bar the littlest children. There is an ayah hierarchy, a guard hierarchy, the riots and rebellions of the children that merely mirror the reflections of teenagers all over the world. . . . Internal staff egos must be pampered and nursed, politicians must be lobbied, embassy functions attended. The responsibilities are enormous and it's time for a change.

Most of us can function well under pressure for a

174

while but then, when things start to ease a little, we ironically feel the full weight and the full strain the most. I think that, now the project is starting to function reasonably well, this is happening to me. With the retired staff standby flying concession that British Airways have been good enough to let me retain I'll be able to visit often. I have worked hard to ensure that other people are perceived to have higher authority than me and that, quite simply, the project can continue to develop, improve and thrive. Mr Haque runs the project so well now there is often very little for me to do on a day-to-day basis. The objective I have set myself of getting things working smoothly has now been achieved. We are all involved in working out the future development of our programmes and, though this does not need me to be in Bangladesh all the time, I am still very much involved in planning how the project should progress. We'd like it to become more of a short-stay, educational establishment for rehabilitating mothers with their children. I hope that I can carry on taking an active part in developing the project, its policies and systems in a way that will help it to achieve the very most that our funds will allow.

It's important that staff, women and children learn the all-important lessons of self-respect and self-discipline. I was watching some toddlers playing with a football a few weeks ago. At first they all rushed to be the one to get the ball. Slowly their teachers persuaded them to stand in a circle and throw the ball to each other. They'd never played a structured game before, and never learned the fundamental discipline necessary so that everyone could join in and have a turn. If, on the project, we are always fair and children learn that there are places where if they stand in a line their turn will come, they should go out into the world with an inherent sense of the importance of discipline. I think this is one of the most important things the Sreepur project can achieve for the people we reach. This isn't to diminish the importance I attach to attempting to alleviate the suffering of individual destitute children, or hundreds of them, but essentially an extension of the maxim that prevention is preferable to cure.

What will I do? Living in London there is so much to do – the theatre, concerts, supper parties, restaurants. I would love to have the luxury of uninterrupted lengths of time when I could peacefully settle down to re-read Lawrence Durrell's *Alexandria Quartet* then work through a great pile of books including anything Russian and everything by Graham Greene. It's going to be good to see my family a bit more than has been possible these past few years. I've almost forgotten what it's like to feel rested and fit. How to pay for all this is another question. Luckily there are vacancies for occupational therapists at the moment, so I'm going to do some retraining, then part-time work for a while, which will enable me to keep up my contacts with Bangladesh.

Probably I will soon start looking for new challenges. Late in 1991 I was lucky enough to visit Iain, my brother, in Argentina and stayed with him and his fellow researchers in a pretty primitive structure on an Atlantic beach. They were observing whales, and in my borrowed wet-suit I was pitched off their small boat to swim in the icy waters with a whale that seemed to be the size of a DC7. It was terrifying but exhilarating, and not an experience that I would have missed. People go to the movies, read novels, take action holidays to satisfy a basic need for adventure. I've been lucky enough to live one. Adventure isn't always glamorous, but here's to the next one!

Index

Adams, Dicken 51, 55
adoption, international 32
Adrian 9
Alal 129–32
Alison 26–7, 28
Anne, Princess 41–2
Australian High Commission 80
ayahs 17, 27, 63, 82–5, 89, 93, 96,
    110, 112
Azmat 52

Babul 153–5
Bangladesh 31
  climate 64–5, 90, 101–2, 106
  cricket team 106
  cultural differences 34–6, 85,
    112
  cyclone (1991) 1, 37, 106, 162–70
  economy 141
  housing 115
  income levels 115
  international adoption laws 32
  International Aid programmes
    141–2
  war with West Pakistan 107
  women and girls in 33, 113–14,
    115, 133
Bangladeshi community in
    Britain 45
Bell, George 40
Benjamin 28, 64, 91, 98, 100
Bennett, Andrea 42–3

Biba 6
birth control 32–3, 113
Blue Peter 41, 48
BOAC 5–9, 37
Boro Din 117–19
British Aid Guest House
    Association 105
British Airways 80, 136
  Dhaka Orphanage Project
    39–48, 67, 81
  Dreamflight 47
  Operation Happy Child 47
British High Commission 63, 65,
    80, 146
British Overseas Development
    Administration 46

Cambodia 31
Canadian High Commission 80
Care 102
Chalker, Linda 138
Chiswick 9
Christmas 117–19
climate 645, 90, 101–2, 106
Crook, Godfrey 39–40, 49, 51–2,
    54–5, 81
cultural differences 34–6, 85, 112
Currie, Edwina 137
cyclone (1991) 1, 37, 106, 162–70

Daily Express 135
dancing lessons 119–20

Das, Ajite 58, 59
Das, J.K. 25, 58, 151
Davies, James 135
Dempster, Harry 135
Devereux, Gerry 23, 37–8, 39, 41
Dhaka 12, 102–5
  expatriate community 105
  transportation 14–16, 103
Dhaka Orphanage Project 39–48
Dirga Puja festival 117
disaster relief 137–8
disease prevention 96
Dreamflight 47
Dulal 128–9

educational and training
    programmes 113–14, 127
Eid festival 85, 117
El Salvador 31
Elizabeth II 136
Emery, John 80–1
Ershad, Begum 57–61, 80
Ershad, President 81, 98
Evelyn 13–14

Families For Children 14–20,
    22–30, 31
  cultural differences 34–6, 85,
    112
  funding 39–40, 45, 121, 139–40
  sponsorship income 46, 47, 108,
    158
  staff 27
festivals 85, 117
Foyle, Bill 55
fund-raising 39–43, 45, 139–40

Ghislaine, Sandra 78
Gibbs, Colonel 41
Gillespie, Mark 51, 55, 73–7, 79,
    81, 123
Glaxo 106, 164
Gonashasto Kendra 115
Gosling, Ted 38

Haque Mr 71, 76, 92–3, 94, 99,
    112, 155
Hatem 131, 132

Helen 77–8
Hurd, Douglas 137, 138
hygiene 112–13, 125

Independence Day 117
India 31
Indira Road Home 16–20, 23–30,
    38–9, 47
International Aid programmes
    141–2
Islam, K.Z. 52

Judish, Sherrell 17–19
Juil, Mr 128

Kennedy, Sir Frank 53
Kerr, Harry 4, 21
Kerr, Iain 4, 131, 176
Kerr, Pat
  childhood and education 4–5,
    21–2
  future plans 174–6
  MBE 135–6, 137
  occupational therapy train-
    ing 4–5
Kerr, Rosemary 4, 21
Kerr, Vivienne 4, 7, 131
King, Lord 38, 40–1, 43–4, 53, 81
Kurigram aid project 112

Lokhi 150
Lostwithiel 4
Lowry, John 51–5

McDonagh, Maura 43
media coverage 41–2, 44–5, 135,
    139, 174
medical care 122–7, 131
Miah, Tommy 45, 47, 137
Michael and Louise 67–8
Michaelson, Dr 146, 148–9, 150
Mitu 128–9
Monika 144–52
Mother Teresa 12

News at Ten film 42
Nicholas 27, 28

Operation Happy Child 47
Osborn, Mike 171–2
Oxfam 102

Panni, W.A.K. 57
Peter 24, 48
Phelps, Howard 38, 39–40, 49
pilfering 27, 82–3, 96, 110
Puspu 71, 99

Rabia 132–3
rabies 65–6
Rahman, Mr 117–18
Rina 25, 158–61
Royal Maudsley Hospital,
    London 5

Savar Centre for the
    Rehabilitation of the
    Paralysed 3–4
Save the Children 102
Scobling, Ron 40
Shiraz 153–5
Shohel 122–7
Shopna 25, 158–61
Shorala 144–5, 148, 149, 150
Silvester, Trisha 46, 70
Simpson, Lloyd 31
Simpson, Sandra 17, 29–30, 31,
    39, 46, 81, 85, 131, 155
Smart, Ted and Nicky 154
Somalia 31
sponsorship income 46, 47, 108,
    158
sports day 117, 120–1

Sreepur Orphanage 50–6, 62–72
    clothing 106, 108–9
    diet 91–2, 98
    discipline 110–11, 114, 130, 153
    insect life 63–4
    medical supplies 93–4, 106–7
    mongooses 65–6
    opening ceremony 80–2
    recycling 98
    riot 1533–7
    running costs 108–16
    segregation of sexes 53–5, 112
    snakes 65
    staff 85
    volunteer workers 66, 70, 73
    water supply 66, 89, 96–7
Steinkraus, Betty 16–19

Taunton, Claire 57–61, 73–4,
    77–9, 86, 119
Taylor, Valerie 3–4, 85
Terenghi, Airdrie 43, 48

The Visit documentary series 44

Walker, John 106–7, 164
Walker, Malcolm 119
Walker, Marjorie 106–7
Wells, Peter 55
What's My Line 48
Wilcox, Desmond 44
Wilkes, Peter 55
Wogan 48, 136
women in Bangladesh 33,
    113–14, 115, 133

If anyone would like more information on the project in Sreepur, to make a donation or, best of all, to sponsor a child please contact:

Trisha Silvester
Chairman
Families for Children UK
PO Box 104
Beckenham
Kent BR3 1AA
United Kingdom

For any other information on all Families for Childrens activities worldwide please contact:

Sandra Simpson
President
Families for Children Int
45 Russell Hill Road
Toronto
Ontaria, M4V 2S9
Canada